GRAND

DESIGN

volume 2

THE

GRAND

DESIGN

volume 2

A SIMPLY STATED, USER-FRIENDLY
GUIDE TO LIVING IN THE UNIVERSE

PADDY MCMAHON

HAMPTON ROADS
PUBLISHING COMPANY, INC.

Cover design by Marjoram Productions
Cover painting by Nick Gonzalez

For information write:
Hampton Roads Publishing Company, Inc.
1125 Stoney Ridge Rd.
Charlottesville, VA 22902
Or call: 804-296-2772
FAX: 804-296-5096
e-mail: hrpc@hrpub.com
Web site: www.hrpub.com

If you are unable to order this book from your local
bookseller, you may order directly from the publisher.
Quantity discounts for organizations are available.
Call 1-800-766-8009, toll-free.

Library of Congress Catalog Card Number: 99-95404
ISBN 1-57174-155-0
10 9 8 7 6 5 4 3 2 1

Printed on acid-free paper in Canada

Table of Contents

Part II

Part III

Introduction

My original intention was to let the material in these books stand on its own and not to bother with an introduction. In fact, I had in mind just to get it all written down and then to leave it among my confusion of papers and, perhaps, sometime after I had passed on somebody might find it and consider it worth sharing with others. Among other things, I felt that this would be a test of the genuineness of the material; if it had a significance for the public generally, a way would be found to put it before them.

For a while I felt good about that approach. From my point of view it had a beautiful and, I now realize, egotistical simplicity. Above all else, it had the great merit, for me, that I didn't have to submit myself to the public in any way, or risk changing the perception that I thought people who knew me might have of me. It was one thing to be an internal radical in my own thoughts, but to be a public radical was something I shrank from. I also didn't want to be classified as a "nut." Most people who know me would regard me as a conservative and definitely a sane sort of person, fitting in pretty well with, and subscribing to, the established order of things. I'm sure they see me as wanting no more than to live a quiet, orderly, comfortably anonymous life; so why would I want to change all that?

Ultimately, I think, the answer for me lies in the fact that I'm part of the jigsaw puzzle of the All, or God, or whatever word can be used to describe totality. I don't exist in isolation. As a spiritual being, by my very existence I'm eternally creative. If my life on Earth is to mean anything I must contribute to the evolutionary and creative process in the best way I can. It seems to me, therefore, that, in a sense, it would be a denial of my existence if I deliberately refrained from sharing with others the knowledge/wisdom/guidance which for some reason I have been privileged to have been given and which I have found indescribably helpful in my own life.

The question of responsibility arises in a double sense. First, much of what is contained in the books cuts across orthodox teaching. What if reading the book destroys somebody's faith (for example, in religion)? Second, how can I be sure beyond all doubt that the material in the book was transmitted to me from a highly evolved source, as claimed, and was not a product of my own imagination? Facilely, I suppose I could say that if reading the book were to destroy somebody's faith then that faith didn't have a strong foundation anyway. Ultimately, though, I have to say that once I accept the line of thinking in the book for myself, all I can do is offer that to other people. If they accept it, or partly accept it, or if some aspects of it cause them to question their own beliefs, then that's fine. If nothing like that happens for them, if they reject it totally, that's fine, too. In the final analysis each person has to take responsibility for himself.

In the long run I have a feeling that orthodoxy and awareness don't, and probably can't, coexist. Orthodoxy may perhaps be likened to the stumbling steps of childhood (although very definitely not to the sense of wonder in childhood). By its nature orthodoxy imposes limitations of consciousness while the free spirit knows no limitation.

On the question of the source of the material as well as the material itself, the simple and honest answer is that I can't be sure beyond all doubt that what is claimed to be so is so. In whatever ways I can, I want to help people to be themselves. If I didn't believe that the material in the books would do that, I think I'd be very foolish indeed to publish them. I have choices, play safe or put my toe in the water. I choose the latter and let the ripples go where they will. In any case, any reader also has choices to accept or to reject.

I think it is probably true to say that we live in an age where we tend to accept only what we can see before us except those things that we are already conditioned to accept. For example, we accept that Australia exists even though most of us have never seen it except on film or on a map. More significantly, many of us accept profoundly mysterious things, such as the existence of God or the transformation of bread and wine into the body and blood of the Son of God during a ritualistic ceremony, even though we have no visual evidence whatever on which to base that acceptance. I don't see myself as being outside this behavioral pattern. Acceptance of the material caused me quite a lot of soul-searching even though I had the advantage of fairly extensive proof of guidance. I had to examine all my previously held beliefs and submit them to as rigorous a process of analysis as I could. I stripped myself to the best of my ability of all conditioning and got myself into a situation of suspended disbelief. In other words, of having no beliefs at all. Then I allowed my reasoning faculty to take over. The net result is that I have come to accept unreservedly the line of thinking in the book and, indeed, it is inconceivable to me now that I ever had any doubts. Once I accepted the material through my reasoning faculty, it became irrelevant for me whether the source was highly evolved, as claimed, or not. For what it's worth, I believe and trust completely that the source is as claimed.

I hope that readers will be helped, as I have been, to see and feel that life based on the simplicity, and yet profundity of love holds infinitely interesting and joyful possibilities.

Since you are reading this, maybe you will take it as a proof that guidance works, that there is a grand design, and that you and I and everybody else are all comprehended by it; and, ultimately, freed by it or, more accurately, helped by it to free ourselves.

Some time ago I was given a copy of a document entitled "The Cathar Prophecy of 1244 A.D." which is included as an appendix to this book. The Cathars seem to have been present in France only. They were condemned as heretics and were harshly persecuted with, apparently, the last of them having been burnt at the stake by the Inquisition at Montsegur, Languedoc, in 1244. They left the prophecy that what they called the church of love would be proclaimed in 1986. The philosophy outlined in the prophecy seems to me to be very relevant to what's happening in the present shifting of consciousness. In any case, I want to pay tribute to the courage of largely forgotten victims of some of the many cruelties that dogmatic people have, through the ages, inflicted on those who professed beliefs differing from theirs.

Paddy McMahon

November 1999

Part I

The Calamity of Human Ignorance

In our decision to discuss in this session what a soul (in spirit) described to you as the calamity of human ignorance, I do not want to give the impression that souls in spirit have all the answers; indeed they don't but they have access to them as they regain their lost awareness. Inasmuch as souls who are going through a human experience find ways of lifting and letting go the veils of illusion, physical death will become a celebratory homecoming rather than a source of distress and confusion and devastating separation which, unfortunately, it often is.

When one looks at the history of humanity it's easy to see how calamity can be an apt description. All through the ages people have sought to impose their views, their will, their way of life, on others; sometimes by force, sometimes by laws, sometimes as the self-appointed representatives of a supreme being, inevitably by fear. Many people have done so, and continue to do so, in order to gain positions of control or influence, and that, at least, however deplorable, is straightforward. The real tragedy is where people genuinely and sincerely believe that they, and only they, know "the truth" and want to make sure that everybody else lives by that truth. That's the most dangerous and calamitous ignorance of all and can be testified to as such by the multitudes who have been victims of

1

it. I classify it as the worst type of ignorance because it is so insidious, judgmental, and arrogant in its righteousness.

There is only one truth: God. There's only one true God. These are the sort of factual statements which, without elaboration, contribute to the spread of ignorance because of people's tendencies, albeit understandable, towards confining God within the structures of rigid belief systems controlled by conditioning. However, when it is accepted that God is all and all is contained in God and nothing has ever existed, exists, or will exist, outside of God, it can be seen that there's an infinity of aspects or attributes or, dare I say, truths, in God. For example, each human being is an expression of God in a way that's unique to that person. It's impossible to limit God; therefore it's impossible to limit truth. Anybody who says he knows the mind of God, that he knows truth, is deluding himself. That's why, ultimately, there can never be any absolutes of right or wrong, good or bad. Absolutes only exist through limitation. A person may believe that he knows himself but then something happens through which he reveals himself to himself in a new light; and so the process of revelation continues. People live by their perceptions that are usually determined by their conditioning. If they are open-minded, their perceptions change as their awareness increases. That's the wonder of ever-unfolding consciousness; it's never confined within dogmatic belief systems, it lays down no laws, and sets no limits. It respects the freedom of every individual to live his life in whatever way his expression of God is manifesting at any particular time.

In the long run, it's more dogmatism than ignorance that's the calamity although, of course, dogmatism is a product of ignorance.

Freedom

There has been much written, much spoken, and a lot of fighting over the notion of freedom. The right to freedom is usually regarded as a basic human right. But what is meant by freedom?

It can be safely said that slavery is usually regarded as the antithesis of freedom. It can also be safely said that a slave is not physically free. Slavery is no longer openly practiced in a manner of buying and selling, yet it is still an inherent part of the present human condition. For example, marriage is a common human condition. People decide to get married for various reasons. Men and women have a natural mating instinct that can be satisfied most respectably in the prevailing social climate within the institution of marriage. There is a longing for security, for permanence, for communication on an intimate level, for perpetuation and for children (which may be partly the same thing), for protection, for readily available sexual experience, for conformity, for acceptance as an apparently well-adjusted member of society, or for any of a number of other reasons. I know I might be expected to mention love, but it would, I think, be inaccurate to do so as it is highly improbable that the word love means the same thing to any two people. In any event, a marriage takes place and in due course it is likely that a child or children are born. For the sake of tradition let us say that the father is the breadwinner and the mother stays at home to mind the children and do the housework. As the years pass, the daily grind–in his case of traveling to and from work and getting little personal satisfaction from his work, and in her case of monotonous household tasks and perhaps the isolation of suburban existence and the demands of children–produces in middle and later years, if not earlier, a sense of futility, dissatisfaction and waste. It also produces hopelessness at the impossibility of escaping from the burden that had been placed on them other than by dying, which is not a welcome alternative. Under all the frustration there's a feeling that life should have more to offer than this.

There's no point in trying to overlook the fact that the scenario I have described is a common feature of modern civilization. I have taken the example of a married couple as being the most usual human condition. But, of course, many people who are not married exist under conditions that provide their own form of slavery. The person who spends many years caring for an aged parent, the religious struggling under a rule of celibacy, the child oppressed by the demands of school or the home environment, these are but some of many examples. Other forms of slavery are not exclusively confined to the married or single states; for example, alcoholism, gambling, cigarette smoking, drug addiction, promiscuity, disability, illness, single-minded devotion to a cause. You may well ask is there anybody at all in the human condition who is not a slave? What about you trying to put words on my thoughts? Devotion to a cause!

The only answer I can give is that a person is what he thinks, not what he thinks he is. If you think positive, you are positive, if you think free, you are free. How about a person in prison? What good will it do him to think free? The only difference between a prisoner and anybody else is that his physical freedom to move is subject to more restrictions. But he is as free as he wants to be in his thoughts. What I am saying is that the only way a human being can be free is in his thoughts. Every physical human condition, without exception, is subject to restriction. But a person's thoughts are exclusively his own. He can share them with others or not as he wants. He may say that his thoughts are influenced by the physical conditions under which he lives; for example, how can he but think bitter thoughts if he is old and alone, abandoned by his family, and with only an old-age pension on which to house and feed himself? I can only say to him that it is his free choice whether he thinks bitter thoughts or not. But as he thinks, so he is. He thinks bitter thoughts, he is a bitter old man. He thinks joyful thoughts, he is a joyful old man. There are many instances of people who live under exactly similar physical conditions but who, because of the way they think, either rise above those conditions or allow themselves to be adversely affected by them.

Freedom in the real sense can never be a matter of nationalistic achievement or the right to self-government or to own property or to practice religion or to marry or to divorce or to vote or to act as you would wish to act at any given time. Those things constitute a physical license within an always limited framework. Real freedom, however, is totally unlimited. It is a spiritual thing, which does not mean that all spirits, even those without physical bodies, are free. A spirit being with a physical body can achieve freedom as well as a spirit being without a physical body; the way to freedom for both is through their thoughts.

Ideally, then, a person should not limit himself by his thinking or, to put that in a positive way, he should free his thinking from all constraints. There are obvious constraints such as bigotry, hatred, bitterness, intolerance, anger, self-righteousness, fanaticism, despair, envy; but there are other less obvious ones such as piety, prudishness, holiness, self-denial, self-glorification, duty, guilt, impatience, anxiety, worry, fear, authoritarianism, desire to be loved, to be popular, to be wealthy, to be famous, to possess or to be possessed, to achieve power or position, to impose a code of behavior or a particular viewpoint, to conform, to be seen as conventional, to be seen as respectable and respected, to uphold tradition, to be sexually attractive, to be sexually potent, to be recognized as a success, to be appreciated, to be praised, to be shown gratitude for favors done, to repay or be repaid debts, to punish, to harbor grievances, to seek happiness in people, places, or things, to escape from a particular situation, to have job satisfaction, to have sexual satisfaction, to be able to buy better clothes or food or a more expensive house or car. It may not be an exhaustive list but it's an exhausting one! What I've been trying to show is that not only the obvious things, but also what might be regarded as normal wishes and urges are all in their own way constraints on freedom, the real freedom of thought, and by their very existence in thought form they present a barrier which blocks off the receptiveness of the mind to other thoughts.

So what good is freedom, then, if it means giving up so much of what is normally regarded as pleasurable? Freedom doesn't mean giving up anything. It means being free of the pressure of anything and everything. It doesn't mean giving up the experiences of living. It means looking at them from a different perspective. It means giving free rein to the unfettered joy of being, knowing that to be is everything. A spirit, part of God, does not need anything; it already has everything. It is free if it will but realize its freedom. The process of realization is the often painful journey that all must travel. It is unfortunate that pain is involved, but it is the nature of spirit that all must ultimately be free which is the supreme consolation. Part of the purpose of these sessions is to help to take the pain out of the journey towards realization and to make it an enjoyable trip instead.

Good and Evil

There is no evil, only apparent evil.

I have given my description of God and I have explained how expression evolved out of God and how the fall from full awareness happened. It was not ever, is not, and will never be possible that any soul could lose its divine nature no matter to what extent it may have lost or may lose sight of that nature. This is the first and most important thing to bear in mind; in fact, it is the fundamental fact about all existence, and if anybody does not know this within himself, or cannot accept it, then the rest of what I have to say will carry no conviction for him.

The fall from awareness, from grace if you like to call it that, introduced a duality into the fallen souls, which was never before present in them. The lure of power, the desire to take precedence over others, obsessions which gave birth to all sorts of attendant corruption, were and are completely foreign to the fully aware soul. This duality has come to be described in terms of good and evil. It is present in every integrated soul that has not yet regained its former state of full awareness.

For me, the words good and evil have been given much too extreme meanings in common usage to express the duality adequately. However, since they are the commonly used words I'll retain them but define them in my terms.

Good is awareness or the state of awareness which each integrated soul has retained or regained, or a combination of both. Evil is non-awareness or the state of non-awareness in which the integrated soul is at any given time. Within those definitions there is good and evil in every soul, even a highly evolved soul who has not yet regained a state of full awareness.

Within those definitions, also, there can be no such being as a wholly evil soul, since the soul on regaining the stage of integration (the second stage) has also regained some of its former awareness.

Obviously there can be no such beings as devils within the commonly accepted meaning of that word. The only souls who can be placed in that category are those in a low state of awareness who wish to keep others at, or bring others down to, their own level.

What constitutes a good or an evil action may not be at all obvious. For example, prayer may be good or evil depending on its usage; apparently good works may turn out to have evil results; equally, apparently evil actions may have good results. The traditional concept of what's good is very often mistaken for the very reason that it limits experience and, consequently, the growth of awareness. It must be remembered that life on Earth was designed as a learning experience. Much traditional teaching has concentrated on good being the avoidance of experience, or "occasions of sin," which results in stagnation and a tunneling of awareness; and, therefore, much greater evil results than might accrue from the performance of apparently evil actions which may lead to an increase in awareness and, accordingly, good.

Objectively, there are no such things as good and evil in the traditional sense. There is awareness and there are different levels of non-awareness; or, put another way, there is full awareness and there are different levels of awareness leading up to full awareness.

Fear

Fear is a condition common to human beings. It takes many forms; for example, fear of the dark, the unknown, superiors at work, teachers, parents, children, dictators, rulers of different kinds, church leaders, clergymen, policemen, authority generally, being thought foolish or ridiculous, notoriety, poverty, illness, punishment both temporal and eternal, cold, heat, being found to be inadequate, not being loved, not being able to love or to show love, loneliness, old age, middle-age, youth, hostility, competition, confrontation, unemployment, employment, being unemployable, not being able to cope with the problems of the day, meeting people, fire, robbery, mugging, rape, intimacy, nakedness, dirt, cleanliness, change, new ideas, idleness, drunkenness, drugs, promiscuity, nonconformity, anger, insects, animals, crowds, open spaces, heights, enclosed spaces, senility, baldness, wrinkles, sleeplessness, dreams, falling, drowning, choking, travel, meeting prominent people or people who occupy important public positions, the future, God, sin, unworthiness, frigidity, impotence, unattractiveness, being considered mean, accidents, failure, unacceptance, unpopularity, gambling, unhappiness, enjoyment, pain, celibacy, marriage, sexual intercourse, masturbation, contraception, abortion, adoption, foster care, bankruptcy, dying, death, blasphemy, irreverence, independence, dependence, children not being successful or breaking with tradition, shame, embarrassment, dullness, loss of liberty, war, Satan, devils, ostracism, rejection, loss of status, infirmity, loss of control, criticism, hunger, childlessness.

It is unlikely that there is any human being, or that there has ever been a human being, who has not known fear.

Fear is, of course, an emotional condition rooted in the subconscious. It is a learned condition stored in a memory bank, which is essentially what the subconscious is. For instance, a child is taught that if he doesn't behave in a certain way in a given situation he will be punished. When that situation recurs he remembers the punishment and its association with the situation, which creates fear in him; this is an automatic response from his subconscious mind.

The human experience produces many occasions of fear (and, of course, many people use fear as a means of controlling others both institutionally and personally). If the soul can overcome fear while being daily subjected to such occasions, it will have derived great benefit from its Earth existence. It's no easy task, I know, but yet, as with everything, there's a simple answer.

You are a spirit being, part of God. There is no other spirit being greater or lesser than you; all are equal in God. God is perfect, infinite, and eternal. Therefore you are perfect, infinite, and eternal. Therefore you are indestructible and your condition of apparent imperfection is only temporary (you are trying to regain your awareness of your perfection). Therefore there is nothing to fear.

If you can accept all that, you might still find yourself with fear of certain situations or people or things but you will at the same time have an awareness that there is basically nothing to fear. This awareness will help you to rise above the occasions of fear and ultimately to exclude them altogether from your consciousness.

Sin and Karma

I want to talk about sin and karma, which are really embraced in the session on good and evil, but which, I think, merit isolated consideration since they are important factors in the beliefs of many people.

Sin is regarded as the performance of an act (thought, word, or deed), or a series of actions, which offends God. Religious authorities give rulings on what constitutes sin. It is believed that only God can forgive sin but many believe that priests are empowered to do so on God's behalf.

There are many definitions of karma so I'll opt for my own. Broadly, I would define it as the effect part of cause and effect. If you act there is a consequence of your action; the act is the cause, the consequence the effect. All your actions lumped together at any time produce a bank of consequences; that's your karma. It's being added to all the time on the credit or debit side, like a bank account. Karma is a combination of credits and debits; sin is all debit.

An important distinction between the two is that by an act of forgiveness on the part of God or one of His agents, a soul is believed to be freed from sin; on the other hand, a soul's karma is accumulated through its own acts. The existence of a personal God, who is an omnipotent Judge, is central to the concept of sin, but not to that of karma.

As I have already explained in earlier sessions, God does not exist as a separate entity in personal terms. Accordingly, the belief in forgiveness of sin by a personal God is mistaken. The whole concept of sin, with its negative connotations, and forgiveness of sin by a personal God is, in fact, a source of obstruction to souls in the context of life on Earth providing a series of opportunities for growth in awareness. If a person believes that if he doesn't commit sin as defined by his religious authority, or that if he spends his whole life committing sin and repents on his deathbed and is forgiven by God, he is assured of eternity in heaven, there is no incentive for him to be other than negative in his approach to life. The emphasis on sin as a means of producing conformity in behavior by stressing things that people should not do, rather than what they should do, has been an effective method of control from an organizational point of view. But life on Earth was not designed as an exercise in conformity and indeed is likely to be of no value as a learning experience if lived in that way.

A belief in karma is likely to be more helpful from a growth point of view. The emphasis is on personal responsibility for one's actions; that can only be beneficial. But generally, belief in karma and cause and effect tends to be inflexible in its approach in that they are seen to be products of an inexorably self-fulfilling law. The sower inescapably reaps what he has sown.

Now I don't want to give the impression that the sower doesn't reap what he has sown. Generally speaking, he does, but not inflexibly. Suppose a man murders another. If he were to reap what he had sown in a literal way he should be murdered himself either in his present or in a future existence, perhaps even by his victim. The Father's design does not work that way, however. The man who committed the murder will be given opportunities to raise his awareness; these opportunities may include his being a victim of murder himself but not necessarily so. The primary objective is to raise his awareness to the point where he sees himself and every other soul in their true relationship in God. The means of achieving that objective are subject to adjustment in the light of his continuing acts of free will; given the existence of free will, the design has to be flexible.

The concept of punishment doesn't figure at all in the design. An act of disrespect on the part of one individual towards another can only happen because of a lack of awareness in the person committing the act. Any subsequent hardships that he has to endure are the effects of further acts of free will on his part and/or learning experiences freely chosen by him in order to raise his awareness.

Examination of conscience is a helpful exercise if done positively. Wallowing in guilt is not only pointless but extremely damaging to the soul's awareness; both because it produces a negative effect on outlook, and it restricts the possibilities of receiving help from guidance by blocking off receptivity to such help. On the other hand, regular analysis of past experiences with a view to learning from them to the benefit of present and future thinking and behavior can only increase awareness. By regular analysis I don't mean repeated analysis; I mean analysis of each day's experiences and then finishing with them.

The idea of absolution from sin can also help the soul's growth if it removes the feeling of guilt and produces a positive attitude towards the future. Most traditional religious practices originated with a positive purpose but, as is common with organizations as they grow in size, the negative deterrent side of things began to be more and more emphasized in order to produce a base-line common standard of behavior.

Freedom from Negative Karmic Effects

I'm using the word "karma" in the sense of effects accumulated during a soul's progress through its evolution since it fell from grace or got temporarily lost. On that basis karma has both positive and negative connotations, although in general usage it seems to have been assigned a negative complexion; thrown into a "sin bin," as it were!

In much of your religious tradition there has been a strong emphasis on sin. God, as the Creator, the Supreme Being, was and still is perceived as having laid down the standards by which people should live. Deviations from those standards were and continue to be seen as transgressions against God's laws and, therefore, attract eternal punishment unless forgiven by God through repentance on the part of the sinner. As has been the way with most human institutions, particularly the religious ones, fear became a most useful controlling instrument for encouraging obedience to "divine law." Thus, emphasis came to be focused on people's perceived faults rather than virtues.

It's helpful, I think, to observe briefly the development into Christianity of confession and penance. There is a neat simplification in it as a system whereby a person decided, according to a prescribed formula, the ways in which he had offended against God's laws, confessed them to a priest, said he was sorry; and the priest, as God's chosen representative, gave him absolution, subject, perhaps, to his performing a specified penitential ritual. The way was then clear for him to go to heaven unless he subsequently committed more sins which he could later confess, provided he wasn't unfortunate enough to die without having made a "good confession."

The emphasis on being good or perfect within a rigid formula of expected behavior inevitably conditioned people to patterns of self-criticism and accrued emotions of unworthiness.

As human evolution moved into the present century, and particularly into the later part of it, confession, which became generally associated with one religious tradition, retained for some its supernatural connotation; but on a wider front began to be replaced by psychiatry, psychology, psychotherapy, and other forms of counseling. There's a big difference, of course, in that counselors do not see themselves as instruments of God's forgiveness, nor do they represent themselves as facilitators of a supernatural or sacramental ritual. However, there's a marked similarity in that both confession and counseling rely on analytical procedures, more deeply so in the case of counseling.

In comparing, to some extent, confession and counseling, I don't want to convey an impression that I'm devaluing either of them. Both have been potential purveyors of hope without which humanity could have been a cavernous experience. Counseling, in particular, has helped, and continues to help, many people to see themselves in a new light, and to deal with heavy burdens of grief, guilt, etc.

My purpose in this session is not to denigrate in any way the efforts of so many wonderful people in helping to raise consciousness, but to highlight the fact that in spiritual terms it is now possible to see how a complete shift in consciousness may be achievable. Since people were conditioned to a "sin" culture it was understandable that, even where there was no longer any overt religious context, counseling practices would focus on what was "wrong" or negative rather than on what was "right" or positive. The trend evolved into discovering and dissecting experiences from a person's childhood onwards which were regarded as "blockages" or generally negative influences. It is important to stress that the admirable overall objective was to eliminate negative effects. Then the person concerned could go on to live in a positive frame of mind.

Here I need to highlight two considerations in particular.

Because a soul, in its continuing evolution towards regaining lost awareness, takes on many forms and has accumulated a vast range of experiences with consequential effects carried through into successive lifetimes, it is ultimately a futile exercise to attempt to reach a comprehensive explanation and understanding of emotional pressures by attributing them to experiences in the present lifetime; they may be reinforced by those experiences, but that's a deliberate feature of the grand design adapted to the person's own choice. Such an exercise is like walking on shifting sand. There's no firm foothold. You may well comment that it's strange that the grand design doesn't provide that you can easily remember all the details of your past lives. The simple answer is that the burden would be too much for you to carry. You wouldn't be able to function. As you know, it's often a great mercy to forget details of your present life.

Focusing on negativity, albeit with a positive aim, locks people into patterns of consciousness which affect how they relate to the world around them, which in turn, influences what manifests for them in their day-to-day experiences. The ideal way to live, of course, is totally in the moment, free of the past and the future. As you know, spiritually there's no past or future; there's only a continuing present which is how it is perhaps easier to understand that there's no beginning and no end.

The need to eliminate the subconscious may seem to be a somewhat surprising idea in that the subconscious is often described as a source of inspiration. It isn't. Inspiration comes from tapping into the consciousness of the higher self/oversoul, linked to the infinite divine consciousness, channeled, if desired, by guides/guardian angels. The subconscious is the source of fear because it houses emotions indiscriminately. The more you try to live in the past or the future the more you encourage and reinforce the subconscious, and consequently, the more you are controlled by fear. It follows that the more you are involved in a continuing pattern of analyzing the past, the more you are creating conditions for you to exist fearfully. Therefore, you create conditions that control your future because your today is also your tomorrow as well as your yesterday. The vibrations you send out are constantly creating what transpires for you.

Life, whether in spirit or on Earth, essentially the same thing, is continually evolving. Each development, new in its "time," is a stepping stone to another, and so on, which is how stagnation is spiritually restricting. Thus, confession served its purpose at a particular stage in consciousness as also did counseling in its purely analytical form. Now, the surge of life, a reclaiming of divinity, is demanding something more.

I'd like to interject the analogy of a stream into which a big rock or boulder falls. The rock interrupts the flow of the water and slows it down but it doesn't stop it. When the water gets past the rock, notably without needing to confront it or remove it, it gathers strength increasingly and ignores obstacles in its way; rather than having to stop to negotiate them, it is drawn unerringly to the sea and is then part of the vast energy of the sea. The little stream is in the mighty sea and the sea is in the stream. The stream continues to flow in its own individual way. When it unites itself with the sea it expresses all its power. Always, in whatever measure, it is water as the sea is.

What's the something more that's demanded? It's the simplicity of the sea being in the stream as the stream is in the sea. Once you accept that through your evolution since you lost your awareness of your divinity you've had countless experiences, thousands of them traumatic and painful ones, you will realize the futility of trying to relive them even in a protected way. In any event, your perception of them as you look back at them would inevitably be different from the way it was when they happened. It isn't possible to re-experience emotions, as you may have found whenever you attempted to repeat pleasurable sensations. There may be similarities but each experience is new.

My message in this session is that the accumulation of negative karmic effects cannot be released through an intellectual or analytical process by itself. You cannot avoid thinking, not that you'd want to. The ideal situation occurs when feelings and thoughts are balanced so that they become a unity. What usually happens because of the ways your cultures have evolved is that thoughts control feelings. Please bear with me to the extent that I'm repeating myself, but it is essential to keep in mind that your awareness is always expressing itself through your feelings and thoughts and that's how you're living and will continue to live eternally; that's what you are.

As you exist in the present moment, the conglomeration of experiences which you have had in all your journeying is of no relevance or importance whatever except insofar as it continues to control your feelings and thoughts; in other words, how you carry the effects in yourself. That means it's of no value to you to try to assess an experience from an objective or standardized viewpoint, for example, whether it was "good" or "bad," in line with a regulated belief system. Examining an experience is beneficial for you only if it helps you to live more positively in the present moment. If you make a value judgment on an experience, for example, by placing it in a "bad" box, you are retaining the effects of it in a negative way in your present awareness. If, on the other hand, you see every experience as a learning or relearning opportunity, without taking up any other position on it, you are undeviatingly on a secure pathway to the total expression of the free spirit that you are.

How can we make the whole process easier? Nobody else can take away your negative karma. For far too long many people in succeeding generations have been suffering under that illusion. But in acknowledging that the key is within yourself, you don't have to set out on a long trail of penitential exercises or extensive soul searching. You can do that if you like, of course, and you'll be helped in whatever approach you take. However, as you know, I'm in favor of simplicity in all things.

In our communication, a central challenge is how to overcome the limitations of your perception as it is within your present human condition. For that reason I referred in Volume 1 to a belief which would be familiar to many people of God as a divinity concentrated in three persons, Father, Son, and Holy Spirit. I stressed that God cannot be identified in personal terms except in the sense that God is present in all persons (as well as in all souls and all life). I thought it might be helpful towards easier understanding to use the symbolism of the Father in terms of those souls who never lost or who have regained their self-awareness, the Son in terms of those souls who are still at the start of the journey or who have not yet mastered the lessons of Earth, and the Holy Spirit in terms of those souls who have evolved beyond the lessons of Earth and who are helping others to find their way; for example, spirit helpers/guardian angels.

In that symbolism, the Father represents the ultimate state of awareness, with the Son and Holy Spirit, while no less divine, representing interim states. In order to give an idea of relative proportions I used a measure of ninety-nine percent to show how many souls are represented in the symbolism of the Father, with the proportion continuing to increase accordingly as souls regain their former state of full awareness.

If I say to you that you are love, that's a statement of fact but it may be difficult for you to see yourself as an individualized entity within a feeling; something that doesn't appear to have substance. I have used the symbolism of the Father, etc., in an attempt to bridge that gap. For example, there are three persons in one God; those three persons represent all souls, so that all are in one and one is in all. Each of us exists only because we are animated by, and linked together in, the loving energy that is God; but it is very important for us to know that we each have our own unique identities which will never be merged into an amorphous non-individualized mass.

I recommend meditation on unity with the Father (in my symbolic usage of that word). It's the simplest and best way of all to obtain freedom from negative karmic effects.

I recommend that you include your guides in the meditation. There is a confusion that seems to exist between the notions of guides and higher self (oversoul, in my terminology). If you look to your higher self exclusively for guidance, you are limiting yourself to the extent that your higher self has not fully regained awareness. You wouldn't be on Earth if it had. Equally, your guides, in general, will not have gone beyond the fourth stage of evolutionary growth, in the context of the seven stages. While they have access to the totality of consciousness in ways not readily available to you, they are still not existing fully in that consciousness because they have chosen to remain at an in-between stage in order to help others to "climb the ladder" of awareness faster; to hold the gate open, as it were, at the fourth stage for others to go through to catch up with them.

I am hesitant to use the concept "Father" because of its personalized and, to some, sexist connotation, but it seems warmer than ninety-nine percent, which sounds rather clinical. Ideally I don't want to use words at all and, in fact, I'm not using words; but my concepts have to be put into words since we choose books as our vehicles of communication with those who may wish to read them. As far as I am concerned, one word is as good as another as long as there is a clear understanding of what is meant; which is that the most evolved possible form of union for you to aspire to is with the Father within the symbolism of that concept as I have outlined it. Your guides are helping you to integrate with your higher self/oversoul and together you expand into a merging with the Father, which involves not only a linking in consciousness with your guides as oversouls, but with all oversouls who have never lost, as well as those who have regained, their awareness. What I'm talking about is the fullness of divine expression without any element of unawareness. It means that you are not uniting yourself with the aspects of the soul which are still clouded by negativity as the evolutionary struggle continues. You are in a totally clear space where no vestige of negative influence can intrude.

When I refer to unity with God/love in other sessions, I don't want to create any misunderstanding between the notions of "Father" and "God." It is too cumbersome and perhaps introduces an unnecessary complication to keep saying "God, the Father," which is what is really meant. I have described God as the animating force or energy in all life; nothing exists outside of God. The human being who is engaged in what may seem to be the most depraved of activities is as much a part of God as any of the ninety-nine percent; the all important difference is, of course, that the human has confined his divinity in a prison of unawareness. When you consciously place yourself in union with the

Father you are merging with the fully realized divine expression without being affected in any way by the temporary negativity of the balance of the struggling one percent. If the word "Father" creates any difficulty for you, for example, because of sexist, religious, or personalized overtones, please substitute any word or image that appeals to you as long as you are clear as to what it means to you.

Since nothing exists on Earth without somebody having to do something, an understandable question for you to ask is, what do you have to do if you wish to act on my suggestion of enabling a feeling of unity with the Father (or whatever concept you prefer)? The last thing I want is that you would get trapped by an image created by a particular word or symbol. Words have to be used in our communication in order to create an understanding between us. Now that we understand each other, I hope we can let the definitions go; and I'd like to offer, in greater detail signposts, which I feel can help you reach the desired unity.

1. You don't have to do anything, as such, other than to allow the feeling to happen.
2. As always, the more relaxed you are the better.
3. Sit or stand, whichever suits you, comfortably.
4. Invite your guides to help you and join with you in the exercise.
5. Don't try to visualize or create anything; if images or words flit across your mind, let them be. Because your intention is clear that you want union with the Father, that has been impressed on your consciousness in a linking with the consciousness of the Father and no effort, other than the intention, is needed on your part.
6. Stay with whatever you're feeling. In my view, it's better not to verbalize at all as words are a distraction;

but please don't put any pressure on yourself to avoid using words if they keep coming into your head; the main thing is that you don't set up any resistance.
7. You don't need to analyze or understand anything or force yourself in any way.
8. Surrender completely to your being. Union doesn't have to take any form; it's a feeling which is beyond definition, analysis or thought.
9. Thoughts will wander in, of course, as will sounds; just let them be. They will merge into your experience if you don't try to block them out or sit in judgment on them.

What's new or different about all that and why am I making such a big deal out of it? All your conditioning tends to create complexity. Rituals, rules, regulations, laws, have become endemically human manifestations. What I'm proposing is to get them all out of the way so that there's utter simplicity. Then there's nothing between you and God the Father. Then, automatically, all the negative karmic effects fall away from you. And then, of course, you will be free to be truly yourself; your divine self rejoicing in its integration with your temporary humanness.

That's the something more that's demanded now, to let yourself feel your unity with the Father within the symbolic usage of that word as I have endeavored to express it. In that way you will allow to happen within you a feeling so powerful that all the emotional baggage which you have been carrying will be swept away. As the love of the Father is constantly flowing towards and around every soul in the universe without exception, you will also be linking automatically with that flow and thus helping in the best possible way all souls who are still controlled by negative karmic effects.

Possession, Exorcism, and Earthbound Spirits

Demon possession and exorcism have been consistently matters of fascination for many people through the centuries. The belief is that a spirit, usually regarded as evil, takes possession of a human being and influences his behavior; and, that the spirit may be forced to leave by a ritualistic practice known as exorcism.

The only demons in existence are creatures of the subconscious. So the first point I will make is that it is not possible for anybody to be possessed by a devil since there is no such being as a devil or evil spirit.

There are, of course, souls at low levels of awareness who act mischievously and often maliciously towards others. This is as true of the spirit world as it is of Earth. Souls in spirit try to influence souls temporarily living as human beings on Earth as, indeed, human beings try to influence souls in spirit (notably by prayer). There is constant interaction between souls irrespective of whether they are in spirit or on Earth. The only difference is that the influence being used by a spirit source is usually not obvious to human beings.

All forms of influence in the sense of imposition or attempted imposition of one will on another or others are expressions of non-awareness (or evil, if you want to be dramatic about it).

It is not possible for any other soul to take over the body of a human being from the occupying soul. The design of the soul/body relationship is such that once the original occupant leaves it, the body dies. When the soul travels while the body sleeps, it does not sever its connection with the body; it remains connected to the body by what is biblically called the "silver cord," which is essentially a connection of light. When the soul decides to leave the body ("death"), the connection is broken.

So what's to stop another spirit from getting into a body while the occupant is off on its travels and the body is asleep? The connection between the soul and the body is sensitive to any invading vibration (like a perfect burglar alarm!) and it is simply not possible for any other soul to take possession of the body while the connection remains unbroken. Could the other soul not break the connection and thus get in? No. Once the connection is broken the body dies. This raises another question; are some deaths caused by invading souls trying to take over bodies? No. This possibility was foreseen when the grand design was formulated. Such an arbitrary or random possibility would have introduced a measure of chance or accident into the implementation of the design and would have frustrated, or at least delayed, its fulfillment beyond the level of delay inevitably involved in the vagaries of free will; and, of course, it would be an interference with the free will of the original occupier of the body if the grand design allowed another soul to take over the body without the agreement of the occupier.

What is called possession is usually agitation of the subconscious, although it is, of course, possible for a spirit entity to control the mind of a human being, if it is allowed to do so. However, as I have said, it cannot take possession of the body, nor can it even share it with the soul whose preserve it is, even if that soul invites it to do so. The design of the body is such that only one soul (mind) can inhabit it, and if that soul decided to leave the body in order to allow another to possess it the body would die. So possession in the sense of physical possession as it is commonly understood is a myth.

Whatever exorcism does or claims to do, it does not drive any alien spirit, evil or otherwise, out of a body.

There are many instances of human beings hearing voices that seem to give expression to malicious thoughts and convey urgings to murder or suicide or other apparently sinister forms of behavior. The voices are not really voices in the physical sense; probably a more accurate description of them would be thoughtforms. They are likely to be projections from the subconscious and/or communications from spirit sources. If the subconscious gains control it may run riot as it often does in dreams; if the control extends into the waking hours, imbalance, which in an extreme form is insanity, occurs. The person who is in a state of imbalance is often an easy prey for an unaware spirit which may well succeed in imposing its will on him and will probably be most reluctant to stop doing so.

A feature of exorcism, as practiced, is that it usually tends to be a lengthy process. It sometimes achieves success for that very reason, because the invading spirit sees no future in staying around and having to endure repeated rituals directed at it. In effect, what happens is that the spirit is persecuting its human victim and now, in turn, it is being persecuted; which, of course, doesn't appeal to it at all!

To some it seems a tidy arrangement that souls in spirit should be in one place and human beings in another, but that's not the way things are. Spirit beings at different levels of awareness are constantly around human beings although they are mostly about their own business and have no interest in, or indeed no consciousness of, what human beings are doing. Some spirit beings, however, remain obsessed with life on Earth for years and they are likely to attach themselves to anybody who will entertain them, in a manner of speaking. Human beings are influenced by such spirits. Sometimes the spirits are acting in what they regard as the best interests of the humans, while other times, of course, they are simply acting mischievously or maliciously.

Souls are free to exert influence in any way they wish. If you allow yourself to be influenced by another or others as to how you live your life, then you are, in a real sense, possessed by that person or persons to the extent that the influence controls your exercise of your free will. It is actually virtually impossible for a soul at the second stage of evolutionary growth to avoid being possessed to some extent in that development of consciousness, either positively or negatively, and depends to a large extent on the interplay of relationships between souls. However, it is desirable that each soul should aim at consciously exercising freedom of choice in all circumstances. The more a soul grows in awareness, the more it will try to help others to achieve that freedom.

But how can, say, an employee exercise freedom of choice in all circumstances since ultimately his employer tells him what to do? The employer tells him what to do, yes, and may even compel him to do, leaving him with the choice of doing or resigning from his job (which effectively may be no choice at all); but he (the employer) cannot control the employee's feelings and thoughts; in other words the employee, if he so wishes, retains complete control over his own consciousness (what he is). Once he knows, accepts, and applies that, he is as free from possession as it is possible to be within the constraints of life on Earth.

The real difficulty with possession is that so many people want to be possessed. They wouldn't think of it in such stark terms, of course. They are looking for affection, for security, or for direction, so it often seems like a great help if somebody takes them over and nurtures them and tells them what to do. This whole area is a minefield; it is particularly so for those who are involved in any form of counseling. Correctly or not, the counselor is generally regarded as knowing more about such questions as how to be happy than the person being counseled. Because of this, counselors may be tempted and pushed into positions where they may give directions to people who are only too happy to accept them. What are counselors to do when people come to them in distressed states, not knowing what to do with their lives, and looking for direction? It seems to me that the more aware counselors are, they can only take one approach if they are to be true to themselves; that is, to help people to find their own answers within themselves.

So where does this leave me with my constant emphasis on the desirability of seeking help from guides in all circumstances? Each soul is a universe in itself; it has everything within itself. When a soul asks its guide for help, that help is provided in a way which is consistent with the soul's purpose of reaching further into its consciousness of itself and what it is. Thus, a soul by seeking help from its guides is, in fact, tuning into its own higher self or consciousness and becoming more and more self-dependent or free of possession.

The traditional polarization of good and evil has colored people's thinking and created an attitude of hostility towards earthbound souls. In reality, of course, they are very much in need of help, and they are, in fact, often helped through their continued contact with human beings.

To anybody who accepts that he has guides, I would strongly recommend that he ask them, if he has not already done so, not to allow any earthbound soul to invade his thoughts. Remember that the guides cannot interfere unless they are asked to do so. At the same time he can, if he so wishes, ask his guides to help him to use every opportunity to help any earthbound souls who might come to him, irrespective of whether they come for positive or negative reasons. It will be a team effort, of course, and the guides will themselves also help the earthbound souls insofar as they allow themselves to be helped. In my view, this is the best any human being can do for his fellow souls in spirit.

What I want to emphasize most in this session is that all earthbound or unaware souls need to be treasured and loved rather than banished. If you reject any soul, again to be dramatic, if you cast it into outer darkness, you are not being true to yourself (love) and are, in fact, separating yourself from life. Bear in mind, however, that you can only offer love; or, I should say, be love, which means having total respect for the free will of each and every soul with whom you come into contact.

You may find it helpful to look at yourself in terms of how possessing or possessed you are by asking yourself such questions as:

How much do you try to influence the behavior of others towards conforming with your own ideas as to how they should behave?

How much do you allow your own feelings and thoughts to be influenced by others?

How free do you feel?

How accepting are you of everybody's right to exercise free will?

Do you expect somebody else to make you happy?

Do you regard yourself as the source of somebody else's happiness?

Do you consider that you have a duty/right to control another/others?

Do you see yourself as the moral guardian of another/others?

Do you use your position, for example, of authority, to compel another/others to obey your will?

Do you manipulate another/others to do what you want them to do?

Do you send out negative thoughts, for example, of bitterness, towards another/others?

Do you pray for another/others that he/she/they may, for example, behave in a manner which you think desirable?

As the questioning continues, the thought will, no doubt, strike you that if you are to avoid possessing or being possessed you had better lock yourself up in a room and stay there without running the risk of communication with others; but even that could be a form of possession in your interrelationship with your immediate family or your friends! One can carry analysis to a point of absurdity. As you know, one of the big advantages of life on Earth is that souls at different levels of awareness can interrelate unobtrusively because of the density of the physical vibration. In the interplay of relationships it is impossible to avoid influencing or being influenced, if only by example. So what I would suggest is that the simplest way out of the dilemma of possession is to bear in mind the special place that each soul has in the cosmic scheme of things and to respect each soul's right to fill that place according to its own truth. What you allow to others, of course, allow also to yourself. In loving yourself with all the tolerance and respect that that implies, you are freeing yourself to love others (all others).

Physical Conflict

"There will be wars and rumors of wars" was a safe prophecy if ever there was one. Physical conflict of one kind or another has been a constant feature of human existence. Except in comparatively rare instances, people have not been given to eating each other (physically), but in most other ways many of them behave towards each other, through the abuse of free will, in a much less civilized way than non-humans do.

Basically, as I've said before, it's a question of non-awareness. Only an unaware soul can treat another soul, whether in a physical environment or not, with lack of respect. At the same time it's not a black and white matter. The growth of awareness may very well be helped by extremely unaware behavior. In that sense, physical conflict, including war, may serve a spiritual purpose which, of course, is not the purpose the participants see or intend.

Suppose somebody is about to attack you physically. What should you do? You have only three obvious options: accept the attack passively, run away if you can, or fight back. If you are spiritually aware, what do you think you should do?

You have other options which are not so obvious. Bearing in mind that he is an unaware soul or he wouldn't be on the point of assaulting you, you could send him love, you could try to hold his eyes with yours, you could call on him to stop, and you could try to reason with him. I suggest that all of these options should be tried, and they can be done instantaneously. If they all fail, the best thing to do, in my view, is to follow your feelings in as detached a way as you can. Your feelings (the real you) will tell you the best way to cope with the situation. This may turn out to be the use of physical force to whatever extent is required. Is that not an interference with his free will? No, it's presenting him with a consequence of his act of free will. He is encroaching on your "space," imposing or seeking to impose his will on yours; he has to learn not to do this. It may be that he will not begin to learn it unless the lesson is sharply administered.

You find it somewhat surprising that I'm justifying the use of physical force in certain circumstances. To be accurate, I'm not actually justifying it; I'm saying positively that it may be the best option in some situations. It's important to remember that what matters is the spiritual effect, not the physical one.

So what about wars? One can reason from the particular to the general. Wars usually start because one country or group of countries seeks to impose its will on another. Again, if all other options fail, the use of physical force in self-defense may spiritually be the best means of dealing with the situation.

Does all this presuppose, then, that individuals or groups or nations or alliances of nations, should in their best spiritual interests, seek to increase their capacity for self-defense? If it doesn't, what's the point of saying that self-defense by the use of physical force may be the best option in certain circumstances?

The distinction in terms of awareness is between aggression and self-defense. Aggression in the sense of imposition or attempted imposition of one will on another is always an expression of unawareness. Self-defense, for as long as it is strictly confined to the prevention of aggression, is an expression of awareness. How about the defense of others from aggression? For your answer may I again refer you to the example of guides. Out of respect for free will they will only intervene if asked to do so. I cannot give you any better guideline than that.

Yes, but suppose an old lady is being mugged; a passerby will not know whether she is asking for help or not. In the case of physical aggression such as mugging, it is always reasonable to assume that the victim is asking for help although perhaps not in a position to articulate the request; any passerby who does not try to help the victim is ignoring a valuable opportunity for spiritual growth; this applies equally whether the victim of assault is human or non-human.

In the case of mental or spiritual aggression—brainwashing, for example—the victim may not wish, or be ready, to accept help. It would be an interference with his free will to impose, or try to impose, help on him. I include prayer and spiritual healing in the category of interference. In due course he will become aware that help is available to him in many different forms; one form will appeal to him, he will ask for it in his own way, and he will be ready to receive maximum benefit from it.

Now to answer your questions; if there seems to be a threat of aggression against them the answer is yes. The second question doesn't arise. Of course, there wouldn't even be a threat of aggression if all humans had increased their awareness to the point where they saw each person's free will as sacrosanct; but then physical existence on Earth would no longer be necessary.

Where does all this leave campaigns for nuclear disarmament, etc.? To the extent that they are seeking an end to aggression on a global scale they are helpful in the spiritual sense.

What about the Christian message of turning the other cheek? This can be a most effective method of self-defense as long as the person using it remains free in his feelings and thoughts, for example, if he does not harbor resentment or hatred. The effect on the aggressor may turn out to be profound.

The physical means used to prevent aggression are spiritually of no consequence or relative importance in themselves. Their only significance is in the effect which they produce both in the aggressor and the recipient of his aggression.

Categorization: Schizophrenia

Each soul chooses to operate primarily through certain qualities which have both positive and negative aspects depending on how well-balanced or unbalanced the soul is. However, because of an overemphasis on a rational or scientific approach, there has been a prevailing tendency to try to put people into boxes or types. This makes for neatness, security; it puts a recognizable shape on the world and everything in it. It is an understandable approach because everything in the physical world has a shape and since the process of thought tends to be conditioned by experience, it only knows shapes and, therefore, limits. What I'm saying, then, is that categorization equals limitation and, ultimately, needs to be avoided. It is, essentially, making judgments.

But surely judgments have to be made in some instances? For example, take the mental condition known as schizophrenia; mustn't it be conceded that certain people at certain times are schizophrenic? And if that is not acknowledged how can they be healed?

Schizophrenia is indeed a suitable example because it illustrates the human condition, The Earth experience was designed because souls had separated themselves from their own divinity. All souls on Earth, then, are to a greater or lesser extent separated from their true selves and are trying to regain their former integration. In its ultimate state of awareness each soul has all the qualities of the whole (God) while retaining its own individual style of expression, which is what makes it individual. What you call schizophrenia is a more extreme form of the separation.

For development purposes it can be useful to highlight the fact that individuals may have chosen to come on Earth with an emphasis on certain qualities more than others; in other words, they can fit into certain personality types. Undue highlighting of those qualities may, however, be detrimental to a person's ultimate growth since the aim is to achieve total integration of self as far as possible, which means that as a person develops it becomes increasingly difficult to fit him into any category or personality type.

Now I'd like to discuss schizophrenia since in many ways it may be the best example of categorization. If you look up the word "schizophrenia" in your dictionary, you will probably find it defined as a mental disorder leading to irrationality, delusions, split personality, or something like that. In my view, medical science hasn't even begun to reach an understanding of the condition and will continue to fail to do so as long as it approaches it in a scientific way.

Being born into a human body is a severe and traumatic adjustment for every soul. Imagine yourself as a bird that can't fly; or as a prisoner locked indefinitely into a cell where there's room only to stand in a crouch or lie down doubled up; or as an avid reader trapped in a long-term situation where you have no access to books; or as a musician who has no hope of finding an instrument on which to play; or as a hopelessly disabled person who can't move; or in any extremely restricting situation, and you will have some idea of what confining the soul within a human body means. Is it any wonder that the body was designed needing sleep so that the soul would have an opportunity to "spread its wings" (in a manner of speaking) at regular, not too far apart, intervals?

Even though each soul has a free choice as to whether it will incarnate or reincarnate in a human body, in the case of some souls, circumstances (the effects of their accumulated experiences on their consciousness) have combined to make it highly desirable that they should attempt the balancing challenge of Earth. At the same time, they know what a struggle it's going to be. They know that, temporarily, they may, through the use of their free will, make things worse rather than better. So it is hardly surprising that they often come in screaming. (It's thousands of times worse than the Monday morning feeling so many people have to endure.)

The whole point of the Earth experience is, as we have discussed earlier, to help souls regain their former integration. If they can get a sense of that integration, even some feeling of it, within the harshly separating conditions of Earth, then they will have achieved a great deal.

Fundamentally, it is ultimately essential that no separation should be felt between God and man, soul and body, spiritual and material or physical. The trouble is that people, through conditioning or otherwise, tend to reinforce the separation; for example, God is seen as a powerful, often threatening, separate Being; to be spiritual one has to reject the material, including sometimes one's own body. There's no proof that there's anything beyond the physical, so if one wants to be obsessive about alcohol, or drugs, or sex, or making money, or any other physical activity, then why not? Obsessiveness, which, of course, is often religiously, as distinct from spiritually, orientated, also tends to be a reaction, or, more accurately, an overreaction, to the conflict inherent in the soul's reluctance, yet a choice freely made, to come on Earth. The schizophrenic soul knows, probably unconsciously, that it needs to be on Earth, but cannot adjust itself to the restrictions involved. On the one hand, it rejects its body, and, on the other hand, seeks to overidentify with it, for example, by excessive indulgence in sex, or drugs, or alcohol, or food.

The difficulty for psychiatrists, psychologists, psychotherapists, or any others who work in what I might generally label as a counseling field is that, wonderfully motivated people though they usually are, they may not fully understand and/or accept who and what they themselves are. "Physician, heal thyself" takes on a new meaning in that context. If they don't, how can they help a more obviously separated personality to integrate itself? Integrate itself into what? The best they can hope for is to help it to conform with what are regarded as the normal standards of society, somebody who "fits in."

The history of humanity shows that throughout the centuries human beings have tended to organize themselves into groups such as political parties, religious organizations, societies, and clubs of various kinds. Each group formulates its own rules of membership and creates its own power structure. A network of security and belonging is thus provided for the individual member, with also, in some cases, a fanatical or obsessive sense of purpose. A common tendency in the groupings is to be protective of their members and ruthless towards those who fall out of line or break the rules, although, depending on the climate of the times, the ruthlessness may seek to be cloaked in a veneer of civilized concern. A person who does not belong to a grouping of some kind is likely to be, or to feel, isolated in some way, or else to seek to create his own sense of status by being deliberately "odd," or radically individualistic.

In my view, because of the human addictiveness to power, status, and exclusiveness, all organizations, *without exception,* are potential vehicles for the reinforcement of schizophrenia or separation. Symptoms, such as unpredictability of behavior, tend to manifest themselves more obviously in those who somehow feel pressurized or isolated by the grouping in which they find themselves.

So what's the best way to deal with schizophrenia or any kind of mental imbalance? Initially, I suggest that all those who are involved in mental treatment (for example, psychiatrists, psychologists, psychotherapists, counselors) should integrate themselves as far as possible, if they have not already done so. By that I don't mean that they have to be perfect; indeed, rather the reverse, since the more they understand and accept their place in the grand design, the more the burden of perfection will fall away and they will realize that they are always in a state of becoming. In any case, it would be impossible for their clients to identify with them if they were perceived as perfect. Once they have dealt with themselves, they know at least what's wrong with their clients and they are treating fundamental causes rather than symptoms. The emphasis in their training on being non-judgmental is of great value. (But how well do they apply that to themselves in their own personal lives?)

The spotlight is now focused on the client. For ease of reference, I'll call him James. The game of life on Earth has become too much of a burden for him. Unfortunately he doesn't see it as a game, so somehow he has to be encouraged to start again, but with a different foundation this time. This means that, in effect, he has to become a child again.

A child sees, touches, tastes, and, above all, feels and expresses its feelings. The process of thought is largely suspended. In James's case, (as in all similar cases), his thought formation has become a victim of his subconscious, so he needs to be helped to create new patterns of thought.

The treatment I would recommend for James, then, is that he identify with everybody and everything within his range of experience from the fresh perspective of a child. This would mean that even with members of his own family he would seek to shed all his preconceptions and look, listen, touch, taste, and smell with new eyes, ears, hands, mouth, and nose. It would be desirable that he should avoid categorization. Seeking to identify things and people by description creates a separation from them. For example, if James sees a tree, he can better identify with it if he doesn't seek to categorize it as ash, beech, etc.; or, if he is listening to music, he separates himself from the sound and harmony and feeling of it if he starts trying to remember its title and who composed it; or, when he meets people, it's much easier to relate to them if he doesn't compartmentalize them as, for example, well dressed, crooked nose, black, white, fat, thin, and thus form snap judgments about them which emphasize his separation from them.

Certain questions ask themselves; for example, how can James be induced to adopt the approach outlined above and, if he does, how can he survive in the everyday world without appearing to be a simpleton who knows nothing about anything? He is a free spirit, an indispensable part of divine consciousness, and it would be an interference with that freedom if he were forced to undergo treatment. Given that he recognizes that he needs help and is prepared to receive it, it would be ideal if treatment could take place in an environment where he would be temporarily free from ordinary day to day pressures and where there would be complete understanding of the process being undergone by him. In a manner of speaking, he has been reborn and the adults around him need to treat him as they would a child.

In my opinion, all forms of mental illness are due to extreme egocentricity; in other words, concentration on the narrow, limited "I," rather than on the universal, unlimited "I." So the ultimate answer is to make the jump from the limited to the unlimited. The jump is a risky one if neither the therapist nor the client has a clear understanding of the unlimited "I."

Giving and Receiving Help; Expanding into Universal Love

What can you do if somebody does not recognize that he needs help and yet is obviously in a divided, or schizoid, state of mind? Primarily, I recommend that you project loving feelings and thoughts towards him. But I would like to develop that answer into a general suggestion regarding giving and receiving help and expanding into universal love.

Stand as still as you can and allow yourself to feel that your guides are forming a circle with you. Let yourself relax into feeling: love flowing round the circle; that the guides are channeling into the circle all the evolved energy of the universe, of God, of which you are essentially a part and which is, of course, in you; that you are accepted and loved totally as you are, without having to put on an act of any kind, and that that love is constant, unchanging, nonjudgmental, unconditional; that whatever burdens may be on you, fears, anxieties, tensions, stresses, worries, pressures of any kind, are lifted from you and the universal love is taking care of them; that the universal love is enabling the total fulfillment of your life purpose so that whatever opportunities you need are manifesting for you, and will manifest for you, in the best possible ways at the best possible times; that you are expanding into, and at one with, the universal, unconditional, love; that you are secure in the feeling of being always guided and protected and loved in a way that's totally consistent with your free will as a free spirit, and that there's never any interference with that free will; and that you are, in fact, unconditional love and, as you let yourself feel that, you accept and love yourself more; and you feel yourself supported in every way by the universal love with the result that you have access to whatever you need by way of wisdom, knowledge, material things, love, and that you are flowing comprehensively with life and with the totality of consciousness.

As you progress with that exercise, which I suggest should be done daily, you will find that a certain suspension of thought takes place, for a little while, which allows you to become absorbed in the feeling of what you are and your place in the cosmic scheme of things. This, in turn, leaves you open to new patterns of thought and to giving more and more expression to your higher self, or oversoul, as I prefer to call it.

The exercise, in itself, helps you to accept and integrate yourself. It also gives you free and unlimited access to universal energy or love. Remember that it's all about feeling, or, more accurately, letting go into feeling; included in that letting go are your conditioned, rational, thought processes.

I suggest that you extend the exercise to include in the circle (through imagination, of course) any person to whom you wish to send love, or any situation about which you are concerned, and, in general, all the souls in the universe, both in physical bodies and in spirit.

As you sit/stand in your imaginary circle and let yourself flow with the feelings of love, it is impossible for you to have any realistic concept of the value of what you are doing in the context of the raising of consciousness, individually, where the sending of love to a particular soul or souls is concerned; and, universally, through the spreading of love around every soul in the universe. Yet I can tell you categorically that if only one person in a thousand were doing that exercise, or something similar, on a regular, (say, daily) basis, the effect would be so powerful that within a relatively short time span in your terms, say, about fifty years, there would be no wars, no crime; the freedom of the individual would be respected, and planet Earth would be a wonderfully harmonious place, with the result that the way back to full awareness would be immeasurably so much shorter and less painful.

It is important to realize that it may take a considerable length of time for a deeply divided personality to be ready to receive help. (Looking for or needing help, and being ready to receive it, are two vastly different things, unfortunately.) That's why I recommend the approach of becoming as a child; children are more ready than adults to receive help.

What else can you do to help? Be patient and wait for an opportunity to present itself. How will you recognize the opportunity? If you trust yourself enough, you will. Trying to be helpful, even with the highest motivation, causes more problems than almost anything else when the person apparently needing help is not ready to receive it. As always, you won't be surprised when I tell you that the ideal thing to do is to hand the whole situation over to your guides and then flow with whatever presents itself.

The skeptic may say that I haven't offered any practical solution, something concrete that one can hold on to, something to do, as distinct from sitting around, feeling and thinking and letting go. What I'm trying to convey is that doing, as commonly understood, is often not doing, or undoing, but a reinforcement of the negative, or subconscious (within my meaning of the word "subconscious"). The only reality is internal. What human beings tend to see as reality is a passing parade of events and things and even human existence, which are replaced and remembered or forgotten, like yesterday or last week or last month or last year. So, if you don't internalize your reality, or, I should say, accept that your reality is internal, it is impossible for you to be yourself; you are mainly living your life as a puppet or an automaton, however successful you may seem to be to outward appearances. The doing follows automatically and at the best times when the (internal) reality is created and accepted.

Shame

Consider an infant. It lives through its feelings, doesn't it? It gurgles, it cries, it smiles, it kicks its feet, it expresses its feelings exactly as they are. It has no fear, its sense of wonder is boundless, everything is possible. But with the passage of time it begins to be influenced by its environment. Its parents'/guardians' belief systems introduce controlling factors. Later on, other environmental influences, such as schools, teachers, peer groups, also contribute towards establishing a particular pattern of thinking in the emerging child, adolescent, adult, so that the feeling infant is submerged in the rational man/woman.

A constant theme running through our sessions is the necessity for each soul to free itself from conditioning. One of the strongest ingredients in conditioning is shame.

What is shame? A common definition would probably be that it is a feeling induced by guilt, or dishonor, or going against customary behavior in some way. But, in my view, shame has nothing at all to do with feelings; it's a conditioned pattern of thinking which imposes itself on feelings and thus creates emotions, or unaware expressions of feelings. An infant, or a very young child, doesn't feel ashamed of, for example, its nakedness, or how it behaves. It only learns to be ashamed of such things because its experiences in growing up teach it to think that way.

Life on Earth is governed by rules and regulations. Each nation/state, each society, each religion determines its own laws, its own rules for living under its ambit of control. The person who offends against those rules, who "sins," is expected to feel ashamed of his behavior. If he persists in offending, he is locked away in some institution, or tolerated as somebody who is not "normal." Sometimes, exceptionally, he is regarded as somebody who has established such a position of independence that he is outside the "norm"; a "character" in his own right.

Sources of shame are extensive. Examples may be: poverty, illegitimacy, nakedness, unemployment, adultery, infidelity, sexual practices, impotence, disability, parents, children, accents, skin color, obesity, alcoholism, drug-taking, incontinence, sexual performance, illiteracy, childlessness, promiscuity, virginity, failure to pass examinations or to succeed at interviews for jobs or promotions, work, level of pay, living accommodation, physical appearance, inability to compete, desertion, bankruptcy, imprisonment, relatives, social status. What all the sources have in common is that their origins derive from the ashamed person's perception of the behavior expected from him by another/others, or his own position within the society in which he lives; in other words, he is controlled by what he thinks about himself and/or what he thinks another/others think about him.

How does one become free of shame, or possible occasions of shame? First, by accepting that the source of shame is thought, the conditioned pattern of thinking that has imprisoned the child growing into adulthood; and, second, by letting go of that conditioned pattern of thinking and learning to trust feelings (as distinct from emotions, such as, anger, jealousy, lust, possessiveness). Where feelings are concerned there are no absolutes, no right or wrong, no good or bad; or, put another way, feelings are the only absolute because they make no judgment, they just are. Judgment intrudes when thoughts take over because thoughts eventually categorize; they only know what they know, which is always limited. There's a lot of progress in being able to say, "I know that I don't know."

Shame is a product of a lack of self-acceptance, including, of course, acceptance of one's body. Your body (as everybody's) is the vehicle which you have chosen to fulfill your purpose on Earth. It is ideally suited to that purpose. As and when you accept fully (through feelings as well as thought) that you are divine consciousness, that God is within, and as you align yourself with that consciousness, it will be impossible for you to be ashamed of yourself. Divine consciousness does not know shame.

Abuse

One of the features of the evolution of life on Earth has been the proliferation of therapies aimed at helping people deal with causes or sources of perceived dysfunctionalism, rather than symptoms. The acceleration of growth in consciousness, particularly in the latter part of this century, has been at the root of that trend.

In earlier times there was a prevailing view that more harm than good could come out of delving too deeply into the whys and wherefores. In that way people could get on with their lives and make the best of whatever fate or a higher power had in store for them. The stones were better left unturned as there was no telling where the worms would go! As so much of earlier conditioning had the effect of making people feel like worms (the worms won't take offense, I hope, since they'll hardly be reading this—not in their present form, at least!). There was, perhaps, more shelter under the stones anyway.

What's the answer? Is it helpful to delve into past experiences in order to heal present conditions? Or is it desirable to forget about the past and get on with life as it is?

If we conclude that delving into the past is a helpful proposition, the question arises as to what constitutes the past. Is it to be understood as the present life, or all past lives as well as the present life, or selected past lives in conjunction with the present life? If it is accepted that reincarnation, or the possibility of reincarnation, is a fact, then it has to follow that the effects of past-life happenings are carried through emotionally into the present life. Yet, generally speaking, people don't remember their past lives and, if they don't, aren't conclusions based on examination of the present life and the effects of its happenings necessarily flawed since there isn't access to enough factual information on which to make judgments? And then, although many people accept the possibility of reincarnation, many don't; and the many who don't include (some) therapists whose training predisposes them to disregard what is outside the boundaries of scientific proof.

Abuse in one form or another is a common feature of life on Earth. Ideally, evolution is intended to operate in such a way that human beings will behave with greater awareness than animals. Unfortunately, the reverse is often the case. As a general rule, animals do not abuse each other. They kill each other, but, usually, for survival purposes only. To say that people who have acted cruelly towards others were/are like animals is a grave injustice to animals. It's a sad fact that the attainment of an awareness level sufficient to enable the operation of free will does not guarantee the exercise of free will in a manner that respects the dignity of all life forms.

Examples of abuse are manifold, such as, torture, both mental and physical, battering, rape, looting, theft, authoritarianism, brainwashing, bigotry, intolerance, direct and indirect forms of control, criticism, fear, slander, starvation, slave wages, sarcasm, miserliness, political manipulation, incest, favoritism in family/employee situations, addiction to drugs/alcohol, sexual harassment, possessiveness. A particularly horrific form of abuse is the rape of children.

Within the many possibilities of abuse that exist it is difficult for any person, impossible, I should say, to avoid being an abuser and/or a victim at some stages in their lives. I'd like to concentrate our consideration on the area of sexual abuse, not sexual abuse in general but sexual abuse of children in particular.

There can be no doubt that some children are sexually abused. Girls are predominantly the victims and relatives or guardians often the perpetrators. Sometimes the victims remember the abuse clearly, sometimes they have only a feeling of it, and sometimes they may block out the memory of it altogether as the only way they can get on with living their lives.

My special concern in this session is about cases where there's no clear memory of sexual abuse. Suppose a woman, due to circumstances in her life, decides that she needs therapy. In the unfolding of the interaction with her therapist her childhood relationships are explored. Obviously, her relationship with her parents cannot but have had significant influences on her conditioning, including her sexual expression. Her feelings about each of her parents are examined. Generally, there was a reticence about sexual matters insofar as both her parents were concerned. She remembers being cuddled by her father, but, at a certain stage, when she was about nine, he no longer made any physical demonstrations of love towards her. For some time she continued to put her arms around his neck or to attempt to sit on his lap but either he pushed her away or her mother gave her something to do to distract her. Soon she got the message.

In the course of the therapy the reasons for the behavioral change on her father's part and also her mother's obvious discouragement of any physical contact between father and daughter are analyzed. A possible explanation could be that her father's cuddling of her was more sexual than parental; that her mother became aware of that and made sure it stopped. That explanation would help to make sense of some of the problems that she has been experiencing in her adult life. However, since she has no memory of anything that might be construed as sexual abuse, how can she find proof of something which is now, to her thinking, moving more into the realms of probability than possibility? An obvious answer is to confront her parents, who are both still alive. She does so. They are horrified and deeply disturbed, and vehemently deny any suggestion of sexual abuse. The resulting situation is that there's now a deep rift in the relationship between parents and daughter.

The question arises as to whether the woman's last situation is now worse than her first. It undoubtedly is, in my view, because she has transferred responsibility from herself to her parents and she will never be able to heal herself without taking responsibility for herself.

I don't want to be taken as devaluing therapy in any way. However, therapists are also human and are limited by their own conditioning. In many cases, the notion of past sexual abuse has proved to be too convenient a solution for present perceived problems.

It may well be that, in exploring childhood and adolescent experiences of a present life, impressions of a previous life, or more than one life, filter through to the surface of one's consciousness; and, if there's no awareness or acceptance of such a possibility, it is, I think, easy to see how those impressions could be superimposed on the experiences and relationships of the present life with resultant havoc. Another possibility is that, say, a particularly sensitive girl will be responsive to sexual tensions between her parents with consequential confusing emotions within herself; a subtle form of abuse which has no physical manifestation.

What I'm attempting to convey in this session is that reaching conclusions from projected and incidentally limited perspectives is, at best, unwise and, at worst, dangerous. All forms of psychiatric, psychological, counseling evaluations need to expand their horizons. In spite of the recent acceleration of growth in consciousness, which is momentously significant and encouraging, humanity, in general, is still in an embryonic state struggling to come to terms with its divinity; as it does, its understanding will automatically increase so that it won't seek to jump to conclusions which may be totally unwarranted and unjust invasions of privacy.

You may ask why is it that, if people carry with them effects from past lives which influence their present lives, the grand design does not provide for even selective memory recall of past life experiences which would be relevant to the present life and assist in understanding it. The notion of reincarnation is offensive to the beliefs of many people and expansion of their beliefs can only come through their free will. For those who believe in reincarnation, or the possibility of it, there's a matter of timing; in other words, the stage of being ready to hear and accept the information. The grand design ensures that people who are open to receive will always be guided to the appropriate sources of help for them.

There are, of course, many instances where people consciously remember having been sexually abused as children in their present lives. We'll consider such cases later.

Reality

In your daily life there's a physical reality for which you need no proof. For example, you live in a house, you sleep in a bed, you wear clothes, you eat food, you drink liquids, you use transport of some kind, you see people, buildings, trees, fields, you are aware of your body. By and large, you take all those things for granted.

There are other kinds of reality which are commonplace to you now; for example, you press a button and you see pictures of people, places, etc., on a television screen; you turn on a radio and you hear voices, music; you go to a cinema and you see a movie in which actors are playing roles intended to present a reality which on one level you accept and on another you know is the product of the imagination of the creators of the movie and the storyline on which it is based.

You accept as reality things that are outside of your personal experience; for example, the existence of places that you have never visited, of languages that you don't know, of planets of which you have only hearsay evidence, of historical events of which you have only read or heard.

Some human beings accept other things for which they have no physical proof, such as the existence of a personal God, grace conferred through sacraments, life after death, eternal reward (heaven), eternal punishment (hell).

As can be seen, there are different levels of acceptance of reality in human terms, some of it unquestioning, and some of it carrying uncertainty in varying degrees.

Please look now, though, at the reality that you accept without question. Everything on Earth has a form or a structure and can be defined in that way. All structures are subject to change so that there is no such thing as continuity of physical form in a static state. It follows that there's no fixed reality from a human point of view. So it's hardly surprising that human beings suffer from insecurity; the human state offers no firm base, nothing which can be guaranteed to remain constant, unchanging. What is seen as reality can have no permanency about it and, in the long run, can only be an illusion.

If, then, there is a constant reality at all, we have to look for it beyond the physical system. How do you create your reality? Through your feelings and thoughts. All creation originates in the mind (soul) of its creator; nothing is built in the external, physical world unless it is first designed in somebody's mind. Even what is accepted as physical reality is different for each person. If, for instance, two people look at a chair, they may agree on its color, its type, its shape, but there are always shades of difference in the way they see it. All souls create their own individual universes, their own reality.

If one accepts that there's life after death, what continues? Not the physical body, obviously, nor any material possessions. The soul continues. What constitutes the soul? Feelings and thoughts; the reality that's created within each person. All that people take with them when their life on Earth ceases is their state of being.

Each soul's reality is uniquely its own, but each soul is linked in consciousness with all other souls in God/love. The ultimate and only reality is in the expression of consciousness in a state of fully regained awareness. Therein lies total security.

Charity

Charity may mean many things; for instance, giving alms to the needy, treating people in a loving, compassionate manner, visiting the sick, the old, the lonely, saying kind things about people, devoting time and energy to altruistic efforts on behalf of others.

There are compulsory (paying of taxes) and voluntary types of charity.

On a global scale there are aid programs for undeveloped countries, and special international efforts during times of crisis, such as flooding, earthquakes, famine.

There are also many agencies operating under the umbrella of providing spiritual help where it is thought to be needed.

From the material point of view, questions such as the equitable distribution of wealth have troubled people through the ages and, in particular, in this century. Communism and capitalism are often seen as the two extremes of differing opinion on this question.

From the spiritual point of view, people individually, and as part of organizations, wish to share their vision of truth with others and, in doing so, often give up much of what are regarded as the ordinary comforts of life, such as material success, home, family.

If there was no continuity of life, that is, if the death of the physical body was the end of life, planet Earth would be a grossly unjust place with some people living under conditions of extreme poverty and degradation, others vastly wealthy, and many at various stages in between the two extremes. Some have all the advantages of modern civilized society, including education, technological aids, comfortable homes, while others are illiterate, primitive, homeless; some have beautiful bodies, others have deformed and ugly bodies; some are born with perfect mental and physical faculties, others are born blind, or deaf, or dumb, or mentally defective; some have outstanding talents, for example in music, writing, sport, others are mediocre or poor no matter how hard they try. It is strange indeed that so many people have believed for so long that an all just God, a remote Being, created man and consigned him to one lifetime on Earth under totally unequal circumstances, judged him on the basis of performance under those circumstances, and assigned him for all eternity to heaven or hell as a result of that judgment. Blind faith may have its merits (although I can't see any) but in what? In whom? Such an unreasoning and narrow view of life is hard to understand.

The logic of the unequal conditions into which people are born becomes apparent when life is seen as a continuing process with Earth as a training ground, and the possibility of repeated Earth lives being open to every soul. In that context life on Earth would have to throw up many combinations of experience if it were to provide effective training.

This, of course, is the reality. In order to be given opportunities to increase their awareness it is desirable that some souls should experience hardship, and some comfort, and all, probably, a combination of both.

Where does charity in its many forms fit into this scenario? This is where I have to become repetitive again. Your guides are aware of your life purpose and the life purposes of those for whom your charitable acts or donations are intended, and will be able to keep you in harmony with the overall purpose. Communication with guidance, coupled with the respect due to each soul as a part of God, will ensure that your charity will never be misdirected. Obviously, kindness to each and every soul is an integral part of that respect. This is the ongoing charity which is a commonplace part of daily living and which becomes an automatic process once there is acceptance of the nature of soul; then what I might call formal communication with guidance will only be needed when exceptional opportunities or requests for charity arise.

Worthiness

What do you deserve? Happiness? What constitutes happiness? Financial wealth? Loving relationship(s)? Good health? Physical beauty? Wide-ranging talent? Fame? Power? Inner peace? Approval by higher power(s)? Record of achievement? Fulfilling employment? Freedom of expression? Spiritual well-being? A combination of some or all of them?

One of the reasons why the evolutionary process is taking so long is that people feel that they don't deserve to be happy. How often do you find that when you're feeling happy you start wondering what's going to be around the corner to change that feeling? It's as if happiness has to be paid for by suffering of some kind; that you're not good enough to deserve it for itself.

Happiness is a feeling. Deservability is controlled by thought that is conditioned by subconscious influences and imposes itself on feeling. From the moment of birth people are classified as sinners, unworthy recipients of God's love.

Even if they're not born into a religious environment, they are still more likely than not to be subject to more criticism than praise.

It's not possible for a person to be happy on a continuing basis without thinking that he deserves to be happy; otherwise he'll think himself out of feeling happy. Rather than let his pattern of thinking impose itself on his feelings, which is the way conditioning works, he needs to allow his feelings to expand his thought processes. Ultimately, happiness on a continuing basis can be a reality only when a soul feels at one with God/love, with the result that feelings and thoughts are completely in balance and there is no conditioned influence.

Everybody deserves to be happy. There can be no doubt about that because every soul is a part of God. It is understandable that souls are imbued with a sense of unworthiness since they deliberately separated themselves from their real selves, that is, God/love in them. Once they allow their own divinity the question of worthiness no longer arises.

No matter what subject our sessions deal with, we keep coming back to unconditional love. There is no other way.

Unconditional Love

We have referred to unconditional love at different times. What is unconditional love? How can one practice it? Better still, how can one be it?

The word "unconditional" means, of course, without conditions: no hooks, no ifs or buts. We have already considered love in detail and have described it, less ambiguously I hope, as feeling and all its expressions, which includes both aware and unaware expressions, and which otherwise I have divided into feeling and emotion, with feeling being the aware expression of love and emotion being the unaware expression.

Love, then, is unlimited expression of feeling in all its manifestations. Unconditional love is unlimited acceptance of feeling in all its manifestations; in other words, whatever the expression is, tolerance, rejection, compassion, resentment, positive or negative, love accepts it as it is, without judgment.

The crunch question is, how does it work in practice? Using the word "you" in a general way instead of the more impersonal word "one," I'll explore the question as best I can.

Suppose you are a parent. Do you expect your son/daughter to behave in certain ways, to conform with certain traditions or social mores? For instance, if they are drug addicts do you accept them? Or if sexually promiscuous? Or in an "illicit" relationship? Or "gay"? Or are resentful of you? Or are uncommunicative with you?

If you don't accept them as they are, you are not being unconditionally loving.

Suppose you are a partner in an intimate relationship, such as marriage. If you find that your partner is having, or has had, an affair with somebody else, how do you feel? Rejected? Hurt? Resentful? Angry? Hating? Did you feel that you loved your partner before you found out about the affair? Has that love now changed to hatred? If so, what was the nature of the love? If you love unconditionally, does that love not remain constant in spite of what your partner may do or have done? If it does not remain constant, it is not unconditional love.

These are but two examples. Others would, of course, also apply, such as relationships within families generally, with friends and acquaintances, with neighbors, in work situations.

If you love unconditionally, then, does that mean that you allow yourself to be treated in any old way, to be just a doormat? Not at all. As we have seen, unconditional love means acceptance of people and situations as they are, without judgment. That doesn't mean that you have to like the people (or aspects of them), or the situations, or that you don't want them to change.

As always, everything—your world—starts with yourself. It is impossible for you to love others unconditionally if you don't love yourself unconditionally. In unconditional loving, acceptance of yourself, it is impossible for you not to have respect for yourself, and in such a way that it is impossible for anybody else to undermine that respect.

So, what happens? What do you do? In the first example given above do you say to your son/daughter, "Yes, it's fine with me that you're a drug addict, or sexually promiscuous, or whatever"? Or, in the second example do you say to your partner, "I don't mind that you're having, or have had, an affair"? No, unconditional love does not demand those kinds of responses. In my view, the type of response that would be consistent with unconditional love would be something like this, "I love you, but I don't like certain things about you, the way you're behaving." You're expressing your position, the way you feel. You're not imposing conditions on the other person, for example, "I love you, but I can't continue to love you unless you change your behavior in the following ways." You're leaving it open to the other person to change his behavior, or not, as he wishes. You're also leaving it open to yourself as to how you'll respond to the change, or no change, as the case may be.

The most difficult challenges to unconditional love come, I think, in the area of intimate, e.g., marital type relationships, since those relationships are particularly subject to intense emotions, such as jealousy, possessiveness, hurt, rejection. Such relationships present wonderful opportunities for growth in awareness. Accordingly, it would be helpful, I hope, to go a little further with the second example where, say, your partner is having an affair with somebody else. Let's assume you have expressed your feelings about it along the lines outlined above. Suppose your partner is not willing to make any change in his behavior. You wouldn't be human if you didn't feel hurt, rejected, resentful, angry. How do you cope with those emotions? How can you transform them into unconditional love? And then, consistent with unconditional love, what do you do?

First things first; you start with yourself. In loving yourself unconditionally you accept yourself as you are, which means acknowledging your emotions. That acknowledgment helps you to deal with them more easily. You understand that those emotions may actually be helpful to you temporarily; but that, in the long run, they can only damage you spiritually. You allow yourself to experience hurt, resentment, etc., but you understand that the real you, the soul/divine you, is not emotional, *cannot*, in fact, be hurt, or resentful, or rejected. So then, once you have acknowledged your emotions and given yourself some latitude with them, the best way to free yourself from them is to let them go into the divine you, or hand them over to your guides, which is, in effect, the same thing. The more you can let go, the more your consciousness merges with the divine consciousness, which, of course, is free from emotions.

And, then, what do you do? Do you decide to stay with your partner or separate from him? If you stay, what form does your relationship take? For instance, if he wishes to maintain his relationship with you while at the same time keeping his affair going, do you continue to have sexual intercourse with him? The simple answer to all the questions is that with the freedom of unconditional love you do whatever you want to do. All the factors which would prevent you from truly expressing your own feelings have been removed.

Yes but, you argue, suppose you have young children and are financially dependent on him, having perhaps given up your own career in order to take care of the children; and suppose you want to have nothing more to do with him; how then can you do what you want to do? If you are truly loving unconditionally, or, more accurately, being unconditional love, that question will never arise. A solution to enable you to do what you want will present itself. That's the way the loving energy of the universe, of God, works. There's no element of chance in it; it's as inevitable as night following day. It's the unfailing way of the universe.

An unavoidable conclusion from what I'm saying is that, if you're in a situation that irks you, that you find intolerable in some way, or even simply that you don't like, it's a sure indication that you're not loving unconditionally. In that case, unless, of course, you want to stay in the situation as it is, I suggest that you look at it, determine what it is about it that you find intolerable, or that you don't like, and then hand it over unconditionally to your guides, divine consciousness, the God within, whichever is most comfortable for you. If you allow yourself to trust in the process with no reservations, no conditions, I promise you that the outcome will be a source of wonder and of joy to you.

As I have stressed repeatedly in our sessions, life on Earth is a platform for growth in consciousness. It is not a law of the universe that growth has to be a painful process. In practice it has been so. Conditioned thinking has tended to isolate humanity into a prison of spirituality or spiritual growth being achieved through self-denial, self-sacrifice, suffering. Once that belief system is allowed to prevail, that's the only way that growth can occur. I cannot emphasize enough that there's another way, a better way. Love does not demand pain and suffering. Enjoyment is central to love. Life on Earth is intended to be an enjoyable experience. If that statement sounds in any way frivolous to you, please examine it. How do you enjoy yourself? Through self-expression; being how you like to be; doing what you like to do. And I'm sure you'll agree that ultimately your enjoyment comes from relating to people in the most loving possible way.

You ask how does one know if one has handed over a situation unconditionally.

I suggest that you ask yourself the following questions: In the handing over process

(a) are you looking for a specified outcome?
(b) are you looking for an outcome within a particular time limit?
(c) are you saying to yourself that because you've been doing everything "right," life owes you what you would consider a favorable outcome?
(d) are you stipulating that you won't be able to get on with your work of, say, service to humanity unless your situation changes in a particular way?
(e) are you leaving the outcome completely open, knowing that, whatever it is, it will bring the best possible solution to your situation in a way which you will find not only enjoyable but better than anything you could have envisaged?

If the answers to any or all of the questions (a) to (d) are "yes," then you know that the process is still conditional as far as you are concerned. If you can give a positive answer to (e), then your handing over is unconditional.

So, then, you have handed over (or turned over, if you like) unconditionally. What next? You still have to go on living your life. How does the solution happen? You are, of course, a participant in the emergence of a solution. You literally "go with the flow," follow your feelings, do whatever feels best to you, constantly reminding yourself of your unconditional handing over of the situation. Life is never stagnant. There's nothing passive about the handing over process. It means aligning yourself with all the evolved energy of the universe in fulfilling your life purpose.

Whatever length of time it takes, realization of a state of unconditional love is the ultimate objective of all souls reaching towards the regaining of full awareness.

Healing in an Everyday World

Healing is a basic need for all people in one way or another. Every human being has at some stage had a physical ailment and/or has suffered from mental stress of some kind.

In the widest meaning of the word, healing is a daily happening for every soul, giving and receiving. A kind word or a smile is healing; treating others with respect is healing; helping others even in apparently small ways is healing. Easing the pain caused to a child by a cut knee and helping to restore his self-esteem after he has been hurt in a non-physical way are both forms of healing. The more a soul is in harmony with life the more effective its healing vibration will be.

However, the word healing has tended to be taken to mean the curing of illness or disability, physical and mental; in this session I would like to discuss it in that context.

The inequalities in the human scene are highlighted by the vast differences in the conditions under which people are born and live. Some people are physically very frail and seem to have no resistance to infections; others are robust and are generally immune to physical illness. Many people are born with deformities of some kind and many acquire them during physical lifetimes; others don't have any physical defects. The inequalities are so obvious that there is no need to go into them any further; and, of course, they are not confined to physical attributes.

It would be impossible to explain in any reasonable way how there could be any meaning to life in the face of all its inequalities if there were no continuity to life. So that's the first step. Once continuity of life is accepted the inequalities can be seen in a different light.

The next step has to do with free will. The soul performs certain actions which bring consequences. In order to make progress along the path of awareness it is faced with certain choices, including the possibility of reincarnation.

If the soul chooses to reincarnate it is again faced with choices as to how much progress it hopes to make in one physical lifetime. If it prefers to move in easy stages or if it has reached a level of awareness where it has only a little more to learn from an Earth experience, it will probably choose a physical body and an environment geared to its needs for that lifetime. On the other hand, if it has many lessons to learn and wishes to try to learn them quickly it will choose a body and/or an environment with many physical limitations.

The key point is that each individual soul chooses its own physical habitat and lifestyle for a particular purpose. The purpose in most cases is ultimately growth in awareness, but it would be a mistake to draw conclusions from any person's circumstances; some souls choose lives of deprivation as a means of helping others, while some souls choose lives of comfort simply because they want that experience. It's a matter of free will.

Now, perhaps, we could look at healing against the background outlined above. The soul chooses a body with, say, a physical limitation such as deafness, possibly for the reason that it wants to develop its capacity for relating to others in a nonjudgmental way. It is born into Earth as, say, a female baby.

It takes some time for the child's parents to discover that she is deaf. When they do, they use whatever means they can to see if the deafness can be cured. Eventually they are told that it cannot, so they try to live with the situation and to help their daughter to do so also. Yet they are constantly hoping that sometime in some way she will be cured; they pray, perhaps they go on pilgrimages, they seek help from healing agencies other than the traditional medical ones. Suppose we take some possible outcomes.

In the first, the child is not cured of her deafness, eventually learns to accept it, and lives a positive and happy life on Earth.

In the second, the child is again not cured, becomes embittered as a result and allows the bitterness to color her whole attitude to life that she endures in a continual state of unhappiness.

In the third, she is cured by one or other of the healing methods and goes on to live a positive and happy life.

In the fourth she is also cured but finds little meaning in her life.

All the above outcomes must be considered in the light of the girl's purpose. It is likely that in the first she will have achieved that purpose, and unlikely that she will have done so in the second. Again in the third outcome she will probably have achieved her purpose, while not doing so in the fourth.

In the second example it is possible that if she had been cured she might have been helped to do better; equally, in the fourth example she might have achieved more had she not been cured.

The conclusion to be drawn, I think, is that healing is neither a good nor a bad thing in itself; it may have positive or negative results. That is why I have already suggested that ideally healing (of a formal kind) should only be undertaken under guidance.

Where does that leave the medical profession and its healing? Again I say that ideally people should consult their guides before going to a doctor; not alone about whether to go, but also about which doctor to attend if there is a choice. A doctor may achieve successful results with one patient and be unsuccessful with another even though both may have similar ailments. The guides, with the soul's overall life purpose as their concern, will know which type of healing will best help that purpose. For instance, a soul may need spiritual healing rather than physical healing; instead of bodily healing, what may be needed is healing designed to help the soul to benefit spiritually from the particular illness which it has chosen. Possibly a psychiatrist or a psychologist or a psychotherapist or a spiritual healer of some kind would be of more help than a general practitioner.

It is believed by some that if the soul is in tune with its life purpose, the body should not succumb to illness of any kind. This is a misunderstanding of the whole design of Earth existence which is to present people with learning experiences in order to help them to increase their awareness. Illness or disability of any kind can be a most valuable learning experience. So can healing or being healed.

Of course, there are many minor illnesses, such as colds, which affect the body. These don't have any significance in the overall scheme of things any more than discomfort which may temporarily be experienced from, say, too much heat or too much cold at a particular time.

In any discussion of illness or disability the question of pain and suffering needs to be explored. Consider, for instance, the sharp pain caused by a toothache. How does the pain arise? Obviously, the immediate source of the pain is a defective tooth. But if the body were dead there would be no pain even though the tooth's condition wouldn't have changed (for a while). Neither would the body experience any pain if it were in a coma, or even just asleep. So it can be said that while the body may be an immediate source of pain it doesn't experience pain. In fact, pain (or suffering) can only be experienced by the mind (soul); in other words, pain is an expression of feeling.

Suppose we take the example of the toothache again. The body, and, to be specific, the tooth within the body, is the immediate source of the pain. We have established that the body itself does not experience the pain but rather the mind that controls the body. It is clear that once the body dies, the stimulus of pain is removed and the mind is, of course, no longer affected. But we also know that the pain from the toothache may be eliminated by other means, such as the filling or extraction of the tooth or the use of medicines.

As has already been explained, the brain is the physical mechanism which the mind uses during an Earth lifetime. It is the sensory link for the mind, its physical agent. So, while it is true in the real sense that pain can only be experienced by the mind, it is more accurate to say, in so far as physical pain is concerned, that it is only experienced by the brain. Thus, once the brain is rendered inactive, for instance, by means of anesthetics, no pain is experienced.

As a general rule, the higher the level of awareness the less pain and suffering there is (unless they are specifically chosen as a means of helping others; for instance, by example). That can be readily seen to be so in the case of mental stress; obviously, if people can find meaning in their lives much stress will be removed. But how does it apply to physical pain?

The brain is linked to all parts of the body through the nervous system. If the mind is at ease this reflects itself on its physical mechanism, the brain, and is communicated through the brain to all parts of the body. Equally, of course, if the mind is not at ease this is also communicated through the brain to the body and causes disharmony, with resultant illness, in the body. Most physical illnesses are, in fact, psychosomatic and that is why spiritual healing can be effective in curing them.

Pain and suffering generally are only of value if they help souls to grow in awareness. I am all in favor of growth being achieved with as little pain as possible. My hope is that these sessions will help at least some people raise their awareness to such a level that they will no longer need pain and suffering.

Overcoming Limitations

How far should one strive to overcome the limitations imposed by Earth existence? If one chooses an environment and general situation in order to strengthen an aspect of soul, is there a risk that by evading those conditions (for example, through being healed of a bodily infirmity) one may be defeating one's life purpose?

Suppose that you find yourself in a position where it is open to you to develop a technique for easy and conscious astral travel, or for healing illness through a form of mind control. What should your reaction be?

None of these things happens by accident. They are all fulfilling a part in the grand design. They are widening the range of opportunities for souls to increase their awareness. However, each soul has its own plan; what may be in accordance with one soul's plan may not fit in at all with another's. So the best answer I can give is that it is always in your best interests to check with your guides whether it is in accordance with your life plan for you to undertake any particular course of development which may come to your attention.

It is relevant to dwell, a little, on the question of healing or prayer in relation to souls in spirit. I would like to comment on some forms of healing, including prayer, directed expressly at souls who have left the Earth scene.

On the one hand, this type of healing may be an expression of concern on the part of souls on Earth for their fellow souls who are no longer physically with them. As such it may be a source of much comfort both to the healers and those whom they seek to heal.

On the other hand, it may be totally misdirected and thus create pressure and confusion for the recipient. A group of souls, say, projecting healing towards a soul without any knowledge of the spiritual needs of that soul may, by the power of the thought forms with which they surround the soul, propel it on a course of action or a line of thought detrimental to the working out of its own unique part in the grand design. People are usually acting for the best, of course, and out of real desire to help others, but they have no concept of the harm they can do in finite terms by misguided acts of good works. I say in finite terms because, as I have already said elsewhere, the grand design is infinitely accommodating and adjusts itself automatically to any setback which occurs in each individual soul's plan. However, if only people on Earth would have enough faith and trust to leave the operation of the grand design to those who designed and those who have agreed to operate it, much faster progress would be made, and there would be much less pain involved in its implementation.

Now I'm not suggesting for a minute that souls shouldn't help each other. Far from it. But if a person gives another person the sort of help he thinks that person needs, he may not, in fact, be helping him at all. Or if he imposes his idea of help on another person against that person's will he is surely not helping him. What part does a desire for power or for recognition play in healing activities?

If you're involved in sending healing through prayer or otherwise to the physically dead, how do you know whether you're helping them or harming them? If you send loving thoughts to them, you're helping them; by loving thoughts I mean messages of goodwill which make no demands, not even to be reciprocated. Alternatively or additionally, if you ask your guides to convey to them your love and to help them in any way possible then, in my view, you're doing the very best you can for them. Ritualistic prayers for so-called suffering souls really only reinforce guilt in those souls if they already feel guilt; the prayers make an assumption of the existence of sin so that feelings of guilt may very well be induced if they are not already present.

Some souls in spirit are in a state of suffering (as on Earth) due to their own levels of unawareness. The souls who operate the grand design are constantly seeking opportunities to help them (without, of course, in any way imposing help). Sometimes these opportunities arise through the coordinated efforts of human beings and their guides (even though, in many instances, the human beings are not conscious of the assistance of guides). The most effective type of help is possible when all involved are working in harmony with consciousness of the part each plays in the work.

Elimination of the Subconscious

Healing is primarily a matter of raising awareness if it is to be effective in the long term. Obviously, then, the elimination of the subconscious (non-awareness) is the most important function of healing.

Analysis of daily experiences in communication with guides is a means of reducing the extent of subconscious control. I would now like to suggest a development of that communication through the following steps:

Ask your guides

1. to tell you what are the areas of subconscious influence insofar as you are concerned. Just ask the question simply and wait for the answer. It will flow in unmistakably in the form of thoughts or impressions, or visual images;
2. to let you know the main area of influence;
3. to let you know how this area of influence originated. The answer may bring you face to face with painful memories, or create in you sensations of discomfort. Don't try to escape from these. Look at them and analyze them objectively and non-judgmentally until you no longer have anything to fear from them;
4. whether that area of influence has been eliminated. If not, repeat the process. If it has, observe the effect for some time (a few weeks, at least) on the way you feel, then ask your guides to let you know the next biggest area of influence and go ahead and get rid of that in the same way.

The first and second steps are easy. Just write down what's given to you.

The third step is more difficult and may take some time to accomplish. I suggest that once you have put the question to your guides you should just wait and an answer will present itself. The answer may be given to you in a dream; or in a visual image while you're awake; or through an experience which would be a reenactment of the experience from which the area of influence originated; or by direct communication from your guides; or by means of counseling. While the methods of providing answers may vary, you can be sure of one thing; they will be given. A person's guides will always find the best way to help him.

The fourth step is again easy.

The higher the level of awareness the less pain and suffering there are. This may seem to conflict with what I said earlier to the effect that at the level of full awareness the sharing of experience is maximized. For instance, the suffering experienced by one soul still climbing the ladder of awareness is also experienced in a very real way by all souls at the top of the ladder, although not in the same way. An apt illustration may be what happens to parents whose child is suffering intense pain; the parents don't experience the child's pain, but their suffering is also intense. If every soul had regained full awareness there would be no pain and suffering. As the level of awareness is raised there will be less occasion for pain and suffering.

Simplicity

There is no truer statement than that life is simple. The trouble is that human beings complicate it. Take a rose, for instance; it buds and blooms, fades and passes on. Nothing could be simpler. And nothing is more beautiful. The nature of being is as the rose. It is an unfolding of love. The bud symbolizes the soul as yet unaware of its own beauty and magnitude. Then the blooming comes as light flows and represents the slow awakening of the soul to its destiny. The fading away is a physical happening which has the appearance of reality but is only an illusion. The inflow of light increases the awareness of love which in turn increases the possibility of simplicity. God is love. We are all part of God. We are love. Nothing could be more simple. It's only when human beings forget who and what they are that complications arise.

Forgiveness

According to some of your religious beliefs, all human beings are born in sin and are only cleansed of their sins and forgiven by God through the sacrament of baptism. Religious ceremonies invariably incorporate prayers for God's forgiveness of sins.

If you feel that somebody has hurt you, rejected you, done you an injustice of some kind, does that mean that at some stage you must forgive that person? Is it, indeed, open to you to forgive? Is there, in fact, anything to forgive?

Everybody in the human condition has felt hurt or abandoned or rejected or betrayed many times perhaps, in their evolution. Occasions of hurt, etc., are present in daily human interaction; a perceived critical word or look, for example, can be a source of considerable hurt to a highly sensitive person. The more sensitive one is, the more likely one is to be open to hurt. Often the person who is deemed to be responsible for causing hurt is quite unconscious of that.

Emotional hurt in its different manifestations, rejection, abandonment, etc., is subjective. What causes hurt to one person will have no effect on another. It follows, then, that people are hurt according to their capacity to receive hurt or, put another way, to the extent that they allow it.

Physical cruelty, of course, causes emotional as well as physical hurt. An obvious example of that is sexual abuse. For instance, how can a child avoid being hurt, or not allow itself to be hurt, by an abusing parent or adult?

I think it's a reasonable conclusion that in some instances, hurt is unavoidable in the human condition. The more a person reaches self-acceptance and a feeling of oneness with God in him, the less possibility there is of his being hurt; his capacity to receive hurt is diminishing in accordance with his increasing feeling of oneness with God.

Even though it's true, then, that a person is hurt because he allows that to happen, it is a fact that nobody who has ever come on Earth, no matter how evolved, has avoided being hurt. So consideration of the question of forgiveness is relevant.

What does forgiveness mean? It may be helpful to use an illustration.

As a child, Helen was sexually abused by her father. In later life there's no question of her being in any doubt about that; she remembers it vividly. She was a young child when it started—only five years of age—and it continued intermittently for several years. Her father warned her not to tell anybody, that it was their secret. Helen loved her father. His approval was very important to her. She had not yet learned what would generally be regarded as acceptable behavior in terms of sexual morality within the particular environment into which she was born. In the earlier stages, the physical pain and discomfort caused by the sexual acts were cushioned by the conspiratorial closeness of her relationship with her father and by the specially favored status which she enjoyed with him.

As she grew older, however, and as she developed into conformity with her environment, Helen became more and more uncomfortable about the situation with her father. She didn't want to risk losing his approval, but she was increasingly in a state of emotional confusion, and the secrecy became a burden of guilt rather than a special feeling of closeness.

Helen's father died when she was ten. His death, which was sudden, deeply shocked her, but, at least, it put an end to the continuing physical situation. The emotional trauma, however, remained with her and affected her in her subsequent adult relationships, particularly where her sexual expression was concerned. For years she suppressed, as best she could, the memory of the whole situation, including the memory of her father; but now she's at a stage where she feels she has to come to terms with it.

Understandably, Helen feels very bitter and angry about the circumstances of her childhood and, in particular, about her father, who was in a position of control over those circumstances. Eventually, however, for her own protection, she will need to transform those emotions into feelings of forgiveness. The question, then, is—forgiveness of whom? An obvious answer is her father, since he was the controller of the situation. But that isn't the answer. What she really needs to do is to forgive herself; that's where freedom for her lies.

You may well ask, "How could that be the answer when she was entirely blameless in her childhood innocence?" She was, indeed, blameless but she took on a heavy burden of guilt which conditioned her into a deep lack of self-acceptance. Accordingly, in her self-expression, she was not free to be truly herself. In a sense, she punished herself for having been a victim.

A soul cannot deny any other soul the right to take responsibility for itself. It's not a matter of choice; the possibility doesn't exist within the expression of God/love.

It may seem strange to say that if Helen feels that she has to forgive her father she's taking responsibility for him. Yet, that's what she would be doing. Her father's motivation in his dealings with her is something for which only he can take responsibility. Certainly, his actions had a profound effect on Helen. The effect remained long after the actions ceased. But Helen must also take responsibility for herself. She was a child, physically powerless to prevent herself from being a victim of abuse by somebody who was in a special position of trust in relation to her; but now she's an adult still controlled by the effects of the abuse. The effects are there in the way she is in herself, how she feels and thinks. That's how she creates her universe. Nobody can control how she feels and thinks unless she allows that to happen. The scope of her actions may be controllable but not her feelings and thoughts. So, if she forgives herself for taking on whatever burden (guilt, etc.), has affected her self-acceptance, she is giving herself freedom to be herself without restriction.

If I may put the illustration into a broader perspective, Helen's journey as a soul seeking to regain the awareness which she lost (as one of the "fallen angels," the one percent) will have operated through many human expressions, some of which will, inevitably, have involved her as an abuser as well as a victim. It is a fact, however unpalatable it may be, that each soul chooses its parents and the environment into which it is born. In its own judgment of itself the soul is choosing experiences designed to deal with recurring effects of other experiences in its continuing evolutionary journey. The likelihood is that the pattern of its evolution is a constantly repeating cycle of experiences and conditioned responses to them. For example, an abuser in one life, a victim in another; it punishes itself for being an abuser (in some form) in one life by being a victim in another. The way of being a victim may not be directly linked with that of the abuser; for example, a murderer in one lifetime may choose a different form of punishment other than being murdered in another lifetime.

It is important to stress that punishment is not imposed on any soul by any external source, such as a judgmental God; it is always self-imposed. Ultimately, the cycle of repeating patterns is only broken when the soul decides that it no longer needs to punish itself; in other words, when it allows itself to forgive itself for all its "sins" of unawareness.

All of us who were the fallen angels seriously transgressed against our own divinity; against God in us. But we couldn't negate that divinity, although, in the process of our transgression, we, through unawareness, did our best to do so. Some of us have already forgiven ourselves for our presumption that we could achieve an impossibility, the destruction of eternal love. (This wasn't what we set out to do, but rather to be the controllers of it; the same thing, since all forms of controlling or seeking to control are ultimately destructive, although, of course, not seen from that perspective by the would-be controllers.)

Mercifully, the grand design protects souls in their progress towards regaining lost awareness from the burden of remembering most of their expressions of unawareness. In my view, it's a masochistic thing for people to try to unearth memories in order to crucify themselves or others, which is ultimately the same thing. As you know, spiritually there's no past; consciousness only exists in the present. Even if you try to recreate a past happening in every physical detail, you cannot, because your present consciousness of it and in it is different; it's like a book, the reading of which gave you great pleasure at one stage and makes no impression on you years later.

In summary, what I'm saying is that forgiveness of yourself for whatever you may have done or not done, in unawareness, is an essential ingredient in unconditional love. Once you have forgiven yourself, the question of forgiving others will be irrelevant; unconditional love means accepting others as they are, so there's nothing to forgive.

Imagination

I want to include imagination in our consideration since it keeps cropping up as, at least, a question mark in the area of communication with guides.

If you look for alternative meanings for imagination you'll find words such as fancy, creativity, insight, inspiration, sensitivity, vision, inventiveness. I've described imagination as the language of the soul, so creativity, insight, inspiration, also seem to be suitable meanings.

People often portray themselves, or are portrayed, as having no imagination. For them, presumably, imagination would be seen to belong exclusively to those involved in obviously creative expression, such as, poets, novelists, script writers, painters, sculptors, inventors, entrepreneurs. But, of course, that's not the case; a soul cannot *be* without imagination.

Each soul creates its own universe; no two souls see anything in exactly the same way. Your imagination is ceaselessly active. If somebody mentions a bird to you, you immediately imagine a bird; similarly with a flower, or a tree, or a ship, or an airplane; no matter what it is, an image of some kind will form in your mind. When you're reading, you're constantly imagining what you're reading. What might be regarded as the most functional of work cannot be done without imagination. For example, a carpenter cannot make a table without imagining it first; neither can a farmer plant a row of potatoes, nor a cleaner clean a window.

Ironically, even though it's true that many people see themselves as having little or no imagination, it is often the same people who will dismiss as "just my imagination" insights and thoughts that come to them "out of the blue"; in the process, they are, at least, acknowledging that they have imagination.

A central difficulty insofar as imagination is concerned is that it tends to be controlled by limitations of what is known. For example, if somebody asks you to imagine a bird, you will create a picture in your mind of a bird that you have seen; or, if somebody mentions an orange or an apple to you, you will picture them as you remember having seen them. Suppose I ask you to imagine being happy; what happens? Or, if you're feeling happy, can you imagine being unhappy? Let's take the questioning a step further. You accept that souls will ultimately regain full awareness and will then have reached a state of total happiness and fulfillment, a heavenly state of complete unity with God/love. Try to imagine how that state might be. The best you can do with it will probably be to equate heaven with your image of complete happiness; and, of course, what happiness means to you is constantly changing as your awareness changes. And that's the way it is. heaven is a state of being which is constantly evolving even in the ultimate state of full awareness.

Heaven is, of course, automatically linked with God. We have discussed God at some length and arrived at a description of God as love or feeling and all its expressions. How can you imagine God, though? You don't have to go looking for an image of God. Wherever you are, God is. In every person you meet, God is. In all life, God is. God expresses for you in all your creativity. In whatever you imagine, God is. So, you see, you don't have to involve yourself in strenuous efforts to create an image of God; all you need do is look around you.

Wherever you are and whomever or whatever you see or feel or hear or touch or perceive in any way you are in the presence of God, within you and without you. In that way your imagination and reality are inseparably linked; in fact, they are one and the same thing. Every feeling, thought, action is stored in divine consciousness; imaginings are, of course, included.

In the nonphysical (spirit) state it's easier to understand the reality of imagination. In the spirit state, creation is instantaneous; all a soul in spirit has to do is to imagine something and it is. It's like having a magic lantern, wishing for something and there it is in front of you. The form will not be material, of course, so whatever you have imagined can be caused to disappear as simply as it has manifested. Imagine how enjoyable the spirit state is when a soul is free in itself; as you know, life on Earth is intended to help it attain freedom.

Meditation: The Material and the Spiritual

If you observe your thinking processes you'll find that random thoughts seem to be going through your head a lot of the time. This is most obvious in meditation when, in spite of the fact that you want to empty yourself of thoughts, they often keep crowding in on you with no apparent order or logic. How does that happen?

Thoughts are a product of the mind. You have found that when you are absorbed in a particular task or subject you exclude all other thoughts from your consciousness without any difficulty. When you meditate you are inclined to drift into a state of daydreaming and thus to become prey to the subconscious part of your mind as happens during sleep; hence the jumble of thoughts.

Daydreaming is variously regarded as timewasting, harmless, relaxing, escapist, mind-clogging. It is often confused with fantasy which is, in fact, something entirely different; fantasy usually involves an exclusive line of thought in a specific direction, whereas daydreaming is formless and scattered.

I have to go along with the view that daydreaming is time-wasting. It may even be worse than that in that it facilitates the spread of the subconscious.

So what's the solution? No more meditation? Meditation is essential towards growth in awareness. I don't mean that it is necessary to sit down or lie down or whatever for a specific period of time each day and meditate, although that may be very helpful. Ideally, the whole day can be a period of meditation through the way in which all its activities are approached.

On the surface there would appear to be good reasons why people have been encouraged to give some time each day specifically to prayer and meditation; the reasons would obviously include trying to ensure that the spiritual side of life is not ignored. Unfortunately, however, the result has been that life on Earth has come to be regarded as a thing of separation between the spiritual and material, whereas the grand design envisages no separation, but rather that the material side of life should be an aid to the spiritual.

The physical body is material. The reason for that is to restrict the soul (the real being) to particular environmental conditions so that it will benefit from them spiritually. The body needs certain material things in order to survive: basically food, clothing, shelter. To meet these needs money is required in the modern world. The acquisition of money has often become an end in itself and in that sense can only fulfill a limited aim, since a person cannot take his money with him when his body dies.

Money and the things that money can buy are all transient and transitional both in themselves and their ownership. This is an obviously true statement, but it is also obvious that many people have difficulty in relating its truth to themselves, and to a certain extent, at least, they let possessiveness rule their thinking. Broadly speaking, society (certainly western society) and its laws are geared towards the preservation and encouragement of the idea of possessiveness.

From the spiritual point of view it makes no difference whether people own property privately or communally or not at all except insofar as whatever arrangement applies to them helps or hinders their growth in awareness. What is particularly important is their attitude to possessions and the extent to which they are free in their minds from possessiveness (of any kind).

It is commonly accepted that a person advances spiritually to the extent that he renounces material interests. Religious orders who cut themselves off from the world, hermits, people who take vows of poverty and/or chastity, are obvious examples of subscribers to this belief. The proliferation of the belief has reinforced the separation between the spiritual and the material in people's minds.

The grand design to which I keep referring is that life on Earth should be experienced, not evaded. The material needs which people have, and ways in which these needs may be satisfied, were specially included in the design so that life on Earth would provide a wide variety of experiences which would help people to grow spiritually. It is quite likely therefore that the person who participates in the hurly-burly of living is in a better position to grow spiritually than the person who cloisters himself off from it.

That brings me back to what I was saying about meditation. The best blueprint I can recommend for living life on Earth in such a way as to gain maximum spiritual benefit from it is to ask your guides each morning to help you to use the day and all its experiences to your best spiritual advantage; and at the end of each day to assess, again with the help of your guides, the lessons and progress of the day. That's meditation (and prayer, also) in continuous unbroken action. If, as part of the day's activities, you find time for specific meditation or prayer, that's an added bonus so long as it fits into the unity of the day and is not regarded as the only valuable activity of the day. I use the words "specific meditation" because, in my view, all meditation should be directed towards a particular object; in other words, there should be a topic for meditation such as unity with the Father, as I recommended earlier, since meditation in a vacuum only acts as encouragement to the subconscious.

Spiritually, no particular activity has of itself greater value than another. Peeling potatoes, typing a letter, digging a ditch, or sunbathing can be of equal or greater or lesser value than writing a poem, or saying a prayer, or looking at television, or collecting for charity; value depends on the attitude with which a person performs the activity. Since each person is a spiritual being, part of God, all his activities are, in any case, invested with spirituality. (As I have indicated in my choice of examples of activities, I mean the word "activity" to embrace what may be regarded as passive pursuits such as sunbathing or looking at television, as well as what would automatically be classified as active pursuits; in other words, each thought, word or deed is an activity.) In essence, therefore, materialism is only an illusion. All life is spiritual and only varies in degrees of spirituality according to awareness.

Unfortunately, a major feature of the separation of the spiritual from the material is that the spiritual tends to have a morose or killjoy aura around it, whereas the material is associated with enjoyment of life. This perception is understandable because of centuries of promulgation of negative dogmas and teachings heavily concentrated on sin (usually associated with material pursuits) and punishment for sin. Heaven would indeed be a joyless place and a place to be avoided if it were to be inhabited by souls at the level of awareness of so many of those who imposed their codes of moral behavior on millions through the ages!

The essence of spirituality is enjoyment. It is a celebration of the joy of being. The aware soul makes no judgments, moral or otherwise, in relation to others. Your guides are not there to inhibit your enjoyment of life or to condemn you if you, say, drink more alcohol than you can soberly hold. (Your body will probably condemn you enough.) Only you, by your own attitude, can separate yourself from the joy of spirit (as distinct from spirits!).

Am I then saying that all things and all aspects of life are there to be enjoyed without inhibition? Yes; but it must be remembered that the aware soul always acts with respect towards himself, towards other souls, and towards all life and all things. If he is aware, he cannot do otherwise.

Random Thoughts

You find that having a specific topic for meditation helps to focus the mind but that random thoughts still keep intruding. How do you stop that happening? Instead of brushing the thoughts aside, try observing each thought as it impinges on your consciousness. Hold it steady without reacting to it in any way no matter whether the thought itself is disagreeable to you or not. After a little while it will fade away. Repeat the process with other thoughts as you become aware of them. Soon you will find that thoughts are no longer crowding in on you and that your mind will grow still. Then you can fruitfully meditate on your chosen topic. After a few meditations done in this way you shouldn't be bothered with random thoughts any more.

If you react to your random thoughts, even by passing judgment on them, which includes rejecting them, you will only encourage the spread of your subconscious and thus retard your growth in awareness.

Prayer

Prayer is, I think, accepted to mean a form of address to God or to some saintly being who is regarded as an intermediary to God. The address is usually couched in formal terms in a format which is in general usage, although, of course, this is not necessarily so.

As a rule it's probably true to say that prayer combines worship of God with specific requests for certain favors. The person praying usually does so in a supplicatory way, on his knees, often with head bowed and hands joined.

The history of mankind shows that prayer to a deity of some kind has been common practice. People have always felt the need for a higher power to regulate the flow of their lives. At times of crisis the need is intensified.

It's a widespread custom for people to pray for their deceased relatives, usually for the happy repose of their souls.

Remember that the person praying is a part of God and therefore an infinity of spirit in his own right. In that light it is meaningless, for instance, to pray for the happy repose of a soul since it is in the nature of the soul to be on its eternally creative way; the last thing it needs is repose in the sense requested.

Suppose you are a father or a mother. One of your children kneels in front of you with head bowed and begs you for a new bicycle. What's your reaction? You're not happy about the child kneeling in front of you and explain that it's not necessary to do so and that you would prefer if he just came to you in a straightforward way with his request. You go on to consider whether it would be wise for him to have a bicycle just now and, if so, whether you can afford to buy it.

Now let's suppose that the child, instead of going to you, goes into a church or kneels down beside his bed and prays to God for a new bicycle. His prayer is heard by his guide (or guides) who applies the same yardstick to it as the father or mother in the previous example. If it seems to be in the child's best interests to have a bicycle the guide will be able to set up a set of circumstances by which one will be made available for him.

In the first example, of course, the child would not have knelt before his father or mother; he'd just simply have asked for the bicycle. Wouldn't it be a much more simple and dignified arrangement if he did the same in the second instance? It would make his guides so much happier if he was aware enough to know about their existence and that they were most eager and anxious to help him.

The drawback with prayer as commonly practiced is that it's a debasing ritual addressed to a remote personal God who doesn't exist in those terms. The prayers are still heard, yes, as in the example given above, and sometimes it's possible to answer them in a practical way; but, generally speaking, they do nothing to heighten the level of self-awareness of the people praying. The gulf in spirit remains unbridged. That's why I place so much importance in regular day-to-day communication with guides. They can give so much help to people, if they are asked to do so, not alone in meeting the daily challenges of life, but in finding meaning in them which is ultimately the only value in having to meet them.

Life on Earth is a learning experience and to be of any value has to consist of a series of challenges many of which are painful. The learning experience can, however, be enjoyable and life can follow a simple pattern if people tune in to their guides and ask for help in coping with and learning from each daily situation. That's prayer made easy and effective.

Apart from the more mundane daily needs, prayers are said for more global needs such as peace or unity. There's absolutely no point in praying for these things. They're already available within yourselves if you will only open your awareness to them.

Communication on what I might describe as a conversational level with your guides is one effective form of prayer. Another which I have already recommended as a big help towards increasing self-awareness is meditation on unity with the Father, with the Father symbolizing those souls who have never lost or who have regained their self-awareness. (In a previous session—on freedom from negative karmic effects—I offered signposts towards enabling a feeling of unity for you.) This is the ultimate goal which all must reach. If you meditate on it regularly you will find it a very rewarding experience.

Repetition of the same words and phrases over and over again is likely to become a mindless ritual for many people, and while it may have value as a form of consolation or hypnosis or self-hypnosis it is not, in my view, helpful insofar as growth in awareness is concerned.

I'm sorry if I'm being very blunt, but I'm trying to take the pain out of the journey towards self-awareness. To my mind, prayer, as commonly practiced, is a form of mental and physical torture and is an abnegation of spirit. Constant communication with guides on a basis of mutual respect and spiritual equality, with a recognition that the guides have reached a higher state of consciousness than the person being guided and wish to bring him up to that level, plus meditation on unity with the Father, again shared with the guides, will enable a joyful unfolding of spirit without any pressure of usage or form or ritual.

You have questions.

How does my statement on God, to the effect that all activities in human existence without exception are animated by the force of love, tie in with saying that prayer as commonly practiced is of no value spiritually? There's no contradiction. Many activities that people engage in carry no spiritual significance in themselves; for example, doing crossword puzzles, or looking at a football match. But the people themselves are spirit beings, part of God, and that very fact invests the activities with the force of love. Such activities are generally recognized as being pleasurable (usually) pastimes and no more than that, and the people are not fooling themselves that what they're doing has spiritual importance.

What about prayers for the development of those who have passed on from Earth? Their own guides and other souls will, of course, be available to help them in any event. If the soul is not prepared to ask for, or accept help, all the prayers in the world won't do any good. In fact they will only achieve an increase of earthbound pressure on the soul and thus hinder rather than help its progress. The best thing to do is to ask your guides to help the soul in whatever way they can. Your concern for the soul, if conveyed to it at the right time and in the best way, may well inspire it to seek help. Your intervention in this way could be very helpful particularly if the soul concerned has a high regard for you.

By putting the matter in the hands of your guides you allow for the use of discretion in approaching the soul concerned. Just think for a minute; isn't it a strange presumption that the God who is supposed to be all-knowing and all-loving needs to be prayed to in order to provide help for a soul which He (I'm using the usual terminology here) loves and knows is in need of help? Help cannot be imposed from outside. The soul has to make a conscious act of will to seek help. That's often the tragedy but ultimately the beauty of life.

Remember that, in the symbolism which I already suggested, if you are communicating with your guides you are communicating with the Holy Spirit. What more powerful form of communication could you have? And why make life complicated for people by imposing liturgies and ceremonies and rituals on them when they have the most effective possible answer to all their needs available to them in the simplest imaginable way?

Guidance in Prayer

I expect that my views on prayer will be somewhat disconcerting.

Every soul has a complete and absolute right to freedom. Prayer may be an infringement of that right in many ways. For example, a person who prays that he may be successful in a competition for a job is, in fact, seeking God's assistance in preferring him over others; or a person who prays that a girl friend/boy friend will marry him/her is seeking to influence the mind of that friend in a way that might not be in his/her best interests; or a person who prays that another might be converted to a particular way of thinking, such as acceptance of a religious belief, is trying to influence that person's right of choice. The fact that prayers may be said with the best of motives is, I'm afraid, irrelevant; no person has the right to decide what's best for another.

If somebody asks you to pray for him, or if you offer to pray for somebody, towards the achievement of a particular purpose, what, in fact, is happening? He is asking you, or you are offering, to use your influence (with God) in his favor. This may well make both of you feel good, but you may, albeit with the best of intentions, be interfering with that person's purpose on Earth.

To take an example; suppose somebody is in bad health. You go to visit him and he asks you to pray that his former good health may be restored to him. You are full of compassion for him and you pray constantly that the burden of illness be removed from him, and you get others to do so also. The man makes a complete recovery and you are all delighted.

Now it may very well be that it's in accordance with the man's chosen purpose in life that things happen that way.

But what if it isn't? Suppose that in opting for an Earth existence the man decided with his guide(s) that he needed the experience of ill health on a continuing basis in order to grow spiritually. Through the power generated by your prayers and the prayers of others you interfered with the man's chosen plan. He is grateful to you now, but what will he feel on passing into spirit again when he finds that you have contributed to the frustration of his life's purpose, even though he has admittedly asked you to pray for him?

In your own case you will have added to the burden of learning which you will have to undertake in the future because you will not be able to see the effect of your actions until later on. Even then you may not be able to accept what you see without having to go through further learning experiences. And what of the others whom you involve in your crusade of prayer?

I hope it is clear why I recommend that prayer should take the form of communication with guides who are in a position to act as channels without interfering with any soul's free will or rights or purpose and who will be able to use the prayer in the best way possible towards the realization of that purpose; and, meditation on unity with the Father.

Again, communication with guides is recommended because there is no way a person living within the constraints of a physical body can see the overall picture in any given situation.

What I have said about prayer can also be applied to healing. I would strongly recommend that healing should only be carried out under guidance. If a person cannot accept that he has guides, I would suggest that before he gives any healing he should ask the Holy Spirit to use his efforts in the best interests of all (which achieves the same purpose in a more formal way).

The thrust of what I'm saying is that people with the most unselfish of motives may quite unwittingly be seriously interfering with the grand design of the Father to the detriment of themselves and the people they are trying to help, unless they avail themselves of the guidance which has been provided for them as part of the grand design.

Exercising Control over Others

There are different ways, including prayer, in which people seek to exercise control over others. I want to explore, in depth, means by which people can protect themselves from such control. I also want to look further into the whole question of communication; not alone communication with guides/over-souls, but also communication between souls in their interaction as humans and as spirit beings, both as between themselves as humans and between spirit beings and humans.

Souls in spirit often seek to control souls who are still in physical bodies. People don't miraculously change when they move from one state to another; somebody who is in the habit of exercising control over others while on Earth will be likely to want to continue to do so after physical death. Accordingly, a human being may have to cope with controlling influences from spirit and physical sources.

The notion of possession figures in any consideration of control from a spirit source. I discount completely even the remotest possibility of possession by way of a spirit being taking over a human's body. The only way that control can happen in the interaction between spirit and human beings is by intrusion into the human's aura or etheric body. In this case, the solution for the human being is to keep his aura clear. How can that be achieved?

If a person can accept that he has guides helping him, he should ask them to keep his aura clear from all negative energies. The guides cannot (in the sense that they may not) interfere with free will; it's not consistent with their state of awareness that they should do so. Requesting protection from them is an expression of free will and allows them freedom to surround their human charge with an impenetrable shield which is only lifted upon request. There's no need to keep on asking; once is enough.

If a person can't accept that he has guides helping him, or if he doesn't believe that they can provide the protection he needs, what can he do? He can regularly cleanse his aura by swirling motions of his hands around his body, using his third eye (center of the forehead) as a base; or he can imagine himself as a cocoon of light colored to his preference; or he can establish a regular pattern of meditation on unity with God/love; or he can free himself as far as possible from all fears, anxieties, tensions, worries, emotional pressures of any kind, through whatever form of relaxation suits him; or he can use whatever other ritual may appeal to him.

In my view, the simplest and most effective way to keep one's aura clear is to ask one's guides to arrange it; there's no point in keeping them unemployed!

Now, suppose that there are some people who feel betrayed by some action or actions of yours and are thinking resentful thoughts about you. And suppose, also, that there are others who feel that you have gone astray somehow in the way you're living your life and are praying constantly that you'll "see the light" and rectify matters. In the first instance, there's a wave of resentful thoughts being directed at you; in the second, the thoughts may be caring, but, of course, the people who are directing them at you have made a judgment about you according to their own belief systems and are seeking to control you within those beliefs.

You may be completely unaware that any of those thoughts are being directed at you; or you may be marginally aware of them; or you may be aware of some of them; or, indeed, you may be fully aware of them.

Suppose, though, that whether you are fully, or partly, or not at all, aware of them, your aura is unprotected; what effect is created on you? You'll find yourself being edgy, irritable perhaps, or depressed, or very tired for no apparent reason, or feeling unwell, maybe, even, becoming quite ill. You'll be more vulnerable to infections and, in the longer term, your physical (and, perhaps, mental) health could be seriously damaged.

If you ask your guides to keep your aura clear, will that protect you from the effects of controlling thoughts being directed at you from all sources, i.e., physical and spirit sources? Most certainly, it will. If you're aware of those thoughts, or, even suspect their existence, you may allow yourself to be affected by them, for example, by feeling defensive or rejected. It's your prerogative (privilege?) as a human being to allow yourself to be vulnerable. But of one thing you can be certain; no external influence will have power to interfere with your life purpose once you have given permission to your guides to keep your aura clear of any such interfering influences.

I cannot emphasize strongly enough how important it is that people should not set themselves up as judges of others. Prayer can be a most insidious form of judgment because it is seen as an act of piety; asking God to make a person see the error of his ways and do what's "right" is a stark example of negative controlling influence. Of course, if prayer is offered in a spirit of unconditional love, that can only be helpful; it's sending love in a totally free way.

Generally speaking, people have little or no realization of the power of thought. Feeling is the source of creation, and feeling concentrates itself in thought which engineers and focuses action. Feelings are expansive, free-flowing; thoughts put structures on them. Everything on Earth is structured; all the physical world distributes itself, or is distributed, into form of some kind. All physical creation exists through concentration of feelings into thoughts on the part of its creators. When one considers the immensity of what has been created in physical terms, one can then perhaps more readily imagine the sheer force of concentrated thoughts directed by a person or groups of people towards another or others.

Language is not a factor in spirit in the same way as it is on Earth. Communication between souls in spirit is rather like telepathy. It is not necessary to put thoughts into a language structure. In the world of spirit, like associates with like. Accordingly, communication is easier. However, growth in consciousness may be much slower in spirit than on Earth if souls are existing in a climate of closed-mindedness. Because Earth is such a dense vibration, the possibility exists of many different levels of awareness interacting, which facilitates faster growth. A disadvantage is that communication has to be articulated, usually, and is therefore subject to misinterpretation.

Souls in spirit seeking to communicate with humans are handicapped by the fact that they are no longer operating within the forms, for example, language, which they used on Earth. At the same time, if they are to make themselves understood, they must find a way of communicating which will somehow fit in with the way of Earth. It's an extremely sensitive business and cannot be achieved successfully without a lot of cooperation at the human end. Something has to be injected into the consciousness of the human recipient which he can seem to hear or see although it's not audible or visible in physical terms. Ideally, the human should be open-minded, tolerant, with no rigid beliefs, as well as being relaxed, patient, and trusting. Being literal-minded or trying to see things in black and white terms is a disadvantage in receiving communication from spirit. It is important to learn to discriminate. Souls are not infallible just because they happen to be in spirit.

How do you know whether you're receiving communication from a spirit source? How can you bring a certainty into it given that it's not possible for a soul in spirit to be present with you in the same way as a human friend would be? The simple answer is that you cannot achieve the same type of certainty as you can, or that you may think you have, in the physical world. Actually, there's no certainty in any continuing sense in the physical world since every body dies and everything else disintegrates. In the long run, the only continuity is in your feelings and thoughts which constitute your consciousness. So the real world for each and every soul is an internal one created by its feelings and thoughts. That world is outside of time and space and, accordingly, is in a permanent state of connectedness in some form with all other individual worlds and with the universe as a whole. Ultimately, the certainty that you think you have in physical evidence is only an illusion, whereas the reality is what you are when you forego all your material possessions, including your body; i.e., your state of mind/soul, which is linked, consciously or unconsciously, with all other souls.

If, then, the reality is soul-to-soul communication, why is it so difficult to establish more clear links between spirit and human beings? I already mentioned the difference between the forms of communication, language structures for example, on Earth as opposed to telepathic intercourse in spirit. The vast difference in vibrations—the heavy, dense vibration of Earth in contrast with the light vibration of spirit—also impedes communication. There are other factors, such as the readiness and capacity of both spirit and human beings to establish links. The challenge for humans is to learn to trust. The human condition exists because souls lost their awareness of themselves, their divine selves. In seeking to regain that awareness they must sometime, somehow, let go of all conditioning, look beyond the narrow confines of the physical world, still the cacophony of energy-sapping thoughts endlessly creating mountains out of molehills, and, in a state of relaxation, trust the insights that, helped by their guides, constantly flow through to them from their linking in with the infinity of consciousness. Shifts in consciousness don't happen unless people are prepared to take risks to develop their intuitive abilities. The rewards are unlimited; literally, the reattainment of the kingdom of heaven within them, or, put another way, letting God happen in them.

Miracles

Miracles are usually understood to be extraordinary happenings beyond the natural order of things; for example, the healing of a person who, according to all known medical tests, was incurably ill. Generally, the reversal of a physical trend or the changing of a physical substance from one form to another is involved; dramatic examples are the raising of Lazarus from the dead and the changing of water into wine at the wedding feast of Cana.

Miracles are often associated with places of pilgrimage. Again the emphasis is on physical healing.

Because most illnesses are psychosomatic, dramatic changes, sometimes classified as miracles, take place regularly in physical organisms. The mind controls the fate of the body. If the mind decides that the body is going to be sick, it will be sick. If the mind decides that the body is going to be well, it will be well unless, of course, it is part of its life plan that it should endure a particular physical deficiency as a learning experience.

You say that nobody can really want to be sick, yet you know that isn't so. How many people use sickness as a means of opting out of situations with which they feel they can't cope? Or as a means of winning sympathy or attention for themselves? Or as a response to a subconscious influence, such as fear?

I will make a very general statement which you may find hard to accept; if healing doesn't happen in the mind it will not happen in the body. It is unlikely that anybody who is ill will admit, least of all to himself, that he doesn't want to be well, that his illness has become a crutch or an obsession with him. So until he finds a meaning in life which will enable him to release himself from the obsession and to convince himself that he doesn't need the crutch anymore, his mind will not be healed and therefore his body will not be healed. Healers or places of pilgrimage may help the mind to free itself with beneficial results for the body.

Take, for example, the case of a woman who is suffering from arthritis and who joins in a pilgrimage to Lourdes. She doesn't profess to believe in any existence beyond that of Earth, and only goes on the pilgrimage out of curiosity, with no faith in any possibility of cure for herself or for others. She takes part in all the rituals and, to her surprise, she finds herself cured of her arthritis. How can this be explained in the light of what I have already said?

The physical facts of the case are simply stated. Before the pilgrimage the woman suffered severe pain and physical restriction from arthritis. After the pilgrimage she had no pain and could move her limbs freely.

The most likely explanation is as follows. The woman had chosen, as part of her life plan, to acquire arthritis and to let herself be healed of it in this way so that she could bear witness to it. Her witness would be all the more effective because of her previously known skepticism. The healing was carried out by her guides and perhaps other spirit helpers. She had already accepted it and willed that it should happen to her.

The whole physical scene was born out of the grand design. As a general rule, there is no interference with what has come to be known as the natural order of things. However, as I keep saying, the design is infinitely flexible and if those souls who are coordinating its implementation consider that an odd miracle will help the progress of the design, then so it happens through specially selected channels, part of whose plan on Earth this will have been. Obviously, if miracles are to have any effect, they can't happen too often or they will be as readily accepted and overlooked as the wonders of nature. Really miraculous events such as the birth of a child or the blooming of a rose have been taken for granted because they are commonplace. But if these things can happen, is it any wonder that other things which are marveled at because of their rarity can also happen? The working of what are deemed miracles is not difficult for spirit. How could it be since all matter is a creation of spirit?

Auras

In the session on the subject of control, I intimated that the most effective way of keeping one's aura clear is to ask one's guides to do so. How, then, is it that, for example, somebody who works as a therapist and who, although she asked her guides to keep her aura clear, was still very much affected by clients, even to the extent of experiencing some of their physical symptoms?

The aura, sometimes called the etheric body, is the spirit counterpart of the physical body. It is a body of light and can be seen as such. It follows the shape of the physical body and when people die they are recognizably similar in their etheric bodies to their appearances in their physical bodies. The aura is really the person in spirit form on Earth so that, in fact, people are present on Earth in both physical and spirit forms. When the physical body dies the aura leaves it and continues to evolve on its journey in spirit.

In case of misunderstanding, I must emphasize that the aura is not the soul; as I have explained earlier, soul is synonymous with mind, through feelings, thoughts, consciousness. The soul can only be seen through taking on form, such as physical, etheric bodies, etc.

People sometimes get lost in complex distinctions between etheric, astral, causal, etc., bodies. That's a way of putting form on levels of awareness or consciousness. It is analogous to, say, hierarchical systems where people, as they move up the ladder, get to wear different clothes. While there are no hierarchical systems in spirit, souls are distinguishable according to their levels of awareness.

The aura foreshadows and reflects the condition of the physical body. Even though the aura, since it is not physical, cannot suffer damage through, say, illness or accidents, it can be affected by such happenings. That's why, for instance, if a person dies in a debilitated condition after a long illness, the etheric body needs a period of recuperation. It's all linked in with the soul, of course; both the physical and etheric bodies are vehicles for the soul, both are affected by the soul's state of consciousness.

When I talk about keeping the aura clear, then, what do I mean? And how can guides do that? Guides don't and cannot interfere with free will. If you decide to run across a busy road without looking to either side of you, you may get knocked down, or cause somebody else to get knocked down. If you neglect your body's needs, it may get ill. If you drink too much alcohol, you may wake up in the company of a hangover. If you take on burdens of guilt, worry, etc., you may feel tired and stressed.

If you ask your guides to keep your aura clear, it gives them freedom to make sure that no spirit being can attempt to control you in order to help you, without interfering with your free will, avoid damage through physical interaction, including controlling thoughts directed at you by a human being.

Let's go back to the case of the therapist mentioned in the first paragraph above. On her request to them to keep her aura clear, her guides would automatically have placed what I can only describe as an energy shield around her aura. The nearest analogy I can give you in physical terms is an electric fence. If a mischievous soul decided to invade her aura, it would receive such a shock that it would immediately conclude, in a manner of speaking, that she was too hot to handle; in fact, all souls coming near her would know automatically that her aura was impenetrable. That doesn't mean, though, that souls in spirit can't communicate with her; they can, but the communication is overseen by her guides who act as filters, rather like secretaries who are continuously on duty and who make sure that she is constantly minded.

While she is still human, she is interacting with other humans on a daily basis. This is in line with her life purpose and, of course, she is affected in one way or another by the people she meets. That's her choice on her evolutionary journey. Keeping her aura clear won't stop her getting tired, or feeling pain, or becoming ill, and won't prevent her body aging and eventually dying; these are the incidental challenges of living on Earth. When she is tired she needs rest; when she is ill she needs healing; when the burden of years lies heavy on her, she needs to be philosophical. If she is doing something, or going into a situation, which is likely to be physically damaging for her, her guides will put opportunities in her way to avert the damage. She may not respond initially to the subtle signals designed to divert her from the situation; if she doesn't, ways of repairing the damage will present themselves to her. Since she has been so aware as to align herself with the evolved energy of the universe, which is the effect of asking her guides to keep her aura clear, she need never fear that she will be neglected, even for an instant.

Part II

Change

Change is a feature of life. The pattern of change is obvious in nature with leaves falling and growing, flowers withering and blooming, season succeeding season, sunshine following rain. It is also obvious in some ways where human beings are concerned; for example, babies growing, physical development and decline, movement from one dwelling-place to another, taking up employment, transferring from one job to another, marriage, retirement, physical death. But change is affecting human beings every day in somewhat less obvious ways; for example, forming of opinions, reading habits, hobbies, environmental developments, religious practices, traveling conditions, inflation, growth in technology, manner of dress, political developments, laws, social movements.

It is commonly believed that as people grow older they are more resistant to change. Various reasons are postulated for this, such as hardening of attitudes, fear of loss of status, the security of the known against the unknown, physical incapacity, doubts about ability to compete or to cope, apathy, a perceived need to protect positions and possessions.

It is, of course, part of the grand design that life on Earth should throw up a continuing pattern of change and, as a result, daily challenges to people, the overcoming of which in a positive way will help them to achieve growth in awareness.

But how does one know whether one is receptive to change, whether one has an open mind or a closed mind? Consider your own case. You adopt a flexible approach to every issue that comes within the ambit of your reading, discussion, or decision-making, and you therefore regard yourself as being open-minded. You have arrived at a philosophy of living that is based on the beliefs that you are a spiritual being, a part of God, that each and every other soul is equally a part of God, that life on Earth is a learning experience designed to help you regain awareness which you have lost, and that you have guides, who are evolved souls who have progressed beyond the lessons of Earth, helping you through your Earth experience. Suppose you have a friend who is deeply religious in an orthodox tradition who argues with you that your beliefs are contrary to church teaching which he outlines, and therefore not only totally mistaken but diabolically so? How open are you to his arguments? To what extent will they change your beliefs? Or suppose you have another friend who goes along with you some of the way but who says that it is not possible for evolved souls to communicate with human beings; that it is only earthbound souls who can do so because of their proximity and affinity to the material conditions of Earth, and that therefore your trust in guides is misplaced. How do you feel about that? You may argue that your friends are entrenched in their views, but so will they argue about you. Do all three of you, in fact, have closed minds, at least in those areas of belief?

If I may carry the questioning a little bit further I'd like you to ask yourself how can you be certain that the thoughts in these sessions are coming from an entity other than yourself? And if you can make certain of that, how can you establish that I am at the stage of evolution that I say I am? And even if you can establish that to your own satisfaction why should anybody else take your word for it and perhaps change previously held views because of what you have written down with imported authority from a self-proclaimed evolved entity?

These are all key questions, some of which we have touched on earlier but which, I think, it would be well to consider in some detail now.

The process by which you arrived at your beliefs was in many ways an exceptional one with a lot of concentrated training that would have produced an unbalanced effect in somebody less well prepared for it. You have now reached the stage where your beliefs are merged with your being, and you would, in fact, have to reject your whole being in order to reject those beliefs. I don't think that's overstating the position. Accordingly, it's not possible for you to accept arguments such as in the two instances I put to you earlier, no matter how sincerely they are presented. All the three of you can do is listen with respect to each other and be true to your own beliefs. That's being neither open-minded nor closed-minded; it's just being, or being true to yourselves, if you want to put it another way.

That's all right insofar as your own personal beliefs are concerned, but it leaves the question of these sessions and, specifically, my part in them still to be answered.

It is, of course, undeniable that I'm a self-proclaimed evolved soul, if I'm there at all! But if I'm not there where has all the material for these sessions come from? Your own imagination is the only possible alternative. Why should you suddenly, out of the blue, get your imagination working at such a prolific rate in a direction which was previously totally outside of your conception of yourself as a writer and, in the case of some of the material (how the whole process of evolution started), outside of your previous range of interests? Also, as you have found, there are times when material flows through to you, other times when it comes slowly, and other times when it doesn't come at all; invariably, you have found, for good reasons. So, at least from your point of view, there's enough evidence to satisfy you that the material is coming from some source outside of yourself.

Now, even if it were possible for me to prove to you beyond all doubt that I am what I say I am, it wouldn't be desirable that I should do so. In the first place, the proof would be exclusive to you alone and any reader of these sessions would be no more advanced from a proof point of view than he is now. In the second place, my hope is that these sessions will present a clear picture and philosophy of life, in all its aspects, which a reader will find reaching him in his inner knowing. If what I have outlined in these sessions is correct, then all the material contained in them is already known to the reader and all I am doing is bringing it to the surface of his awareness; if the material in the sessions reaches him in such a way that he *knows* that it is right for him, then the authorship of the material is of no consequence and, indeed, is irrelevant. On the other hand, if the material is not acceptable to him, it doesn't matter either who or what I say I am, because he's not likely to believe me.

Then why did I do my self-proclaiming bit? My main reason for talking about myself in the first session was, as I said then, for reassurance. It would have placed you in an unfair position and it would have been difficult for you to accept the material if you didn't at least have my assurance that I knew what I was talking about. Any later reference which I made to my personal position was by way of sharing, mainly for illustration purposes.

If I'm what I say I am, of course, the argument that only earthbound souls can communicate with human beings doesn't hold water. Again, I'll have to let the reader make his own judgment from the material in the sessions.

Insofar as change and open-mindedness and closed-mindedness are concerned, the reality is that all souls, young, middle-aged and old, are subject to change and are receptive to it in their own way. It is not wise to make a judgment about anybody else; the fact that he doesn't happen to agree with you doesn't mean that he has a closed mind. Each person can only change at his own pace. The views which he holds may very well be those which are best suited to his present purpose in life; he will respond to other views when the time is right for him. It is *never* a good idea to try to convince another about the rightness of your views; if you have to try, you're doing more harm than good. State your views, if you wish. If the other person is interested he will want to find out more; if not, the subject is best left closed.

Soul Mates

Does each soul (oversoul) have just one soul mate or is it possible that a soul may have a number of soul mates?

By exercising their free will in ways which caused increasing diminution of their awareness, souls placed themselves in states of limitation. As a result, their ways of relating to each other became extremely confused. Thus, in the human condition there have been all sorts of conflicts, cruelties, and misunderstandings. People's abilities to reach levels of intimacy with each other became blocked by fear in its many forms. Yet, sooner or later, each person needs to be able to feel the freedom of revealing himself totally as he is, in an unconditionally loving way, to at least one special other person. And, as he regains his awareness, each person will inevitably find that special other person while they are still in human form.

Because of the vulnerability imposed by conditioning, people have understandably hidden behind defensive, protective masks, which have enabled them to relate to each other and the world around them while keeping their thoughts to themselves if they wish to do so. This can work in the human state due to the density of the Earth vibration. In spirit, however, because of the lightness of vibration, it's not possible to hide one's feelings or thoughts. If a person hasn't found the security of being able to reveal himself while he is still on Earth, he's bound to find adjustment to the spirit (nonphysical) state more difficult since his mask is no longer operable. If, on the other hand, a person has broken the ice by reaching an ease of self-revelation, even if only with one other person, that will have opened the door to his being more comfortable with the process in a more general way, which, in turn, will make his adjustment to the spirit state easier.

An intimate relationship does not necessarily need sexual expression, and may not have any sexual overtones except in the sense that the people involved may be of the same, or different, genders. By soul mates I mean two souls who relate to each other, or more accurately, commune with each other, in a totally intimate way without feeling a need to keep any part of themselves in reserve.

In spirit, in its ultimate state of full awareness, there are no limitations. It follows that every soul (oversoul) can have all the soul mates it chooses to have. While a soul is going through its Earth journey, it's a considerable achievement if it finds one.

Marriage

I'm talking about marriage in the context of a union between a man and a woman, which is given a legal standing, and sometimes a sacramental standing, within communities and national groupings.

Conventional expectation is that partners within a marriage are sexually faithful to each other and do not consider other liaisons.

Societies are built around marriages and nation/states around societies. The ideal is that a harmonious family home is a secure base for the birth and upbringing of children, and for the maintenance of order within communities.

If the possibility of reincarnation is accepted, it is likely, of course, that an individual soul will have, and has had, many different relationships, some of them resulting in marriage. It follows that there can be no such thing as marriage in an exclusive sense, i.e., that a married couple are bound to each other for all eternity. They may wish to have a continuity of relationship, but there's no compulsion in it, no mandatory divine law; there couldn't be, of course, given the existence of free will.

I want to examine the concept of marriage from a spiritual point of view rather than from any standpoint of its convenience as a regulatory form within society.

Marriage, as such, has no special significance insofar as expression of spirituality is concerned. Relationships, including relationships within marriage, do have, of course, great spiritual importance, both in the sense of general contact with the people in one's world, and, also, in more intimate contact with a special other, or others. A person can present a front to the world in general and hide behind an image that he has created for himself, but if he wants to achieve an intimate relationship with another person he will have to let go of his defensive barriers and reveal himself as he is, which includes acknowledging his vulnerability; otherwise the relationship will be artificial.

Marriage, or a marriage-type relationship, brings together two people in a situation where intimacy has to feature in some way. It is essential that at some stage in its evolution a soul should be able to reach a state of total intimacy with another soul and that this should be done within a climate of complete freedom, i.e., with no suppression of personality, no possessiveness, no strings of any kind. Marriage-type relationships allow for that possibility, although, in practice, the interaction of energies within those relationships often causes much conflict, sometimes to such an extent that living together may no longer be spiritually desirable.

It's not possible for me to discuss marriage without putting it into a reincarnational context. The grand design envisaged a vast variety of possibilities whereby souls would get opportunities for growth in awareness; how they availed, or would avail, themselves of those opportunities depends on their use of free will. In their human manifestations people have continually created effects through their use of free will in their interaction with people, which have put them into positions of karmic obligation towards those people. Subsequent relationships between them are designed to clear those obligations. Sometimes, unfortunately, the obligations are deepened rather than lessened, and thus an apparently never-ending cycle of reincarnational involvement seems to exist and the realization of a state of intimacy in relationship recedes into increasing desperation.

As I have intimated in earlier sessions, the grand design moved into a new phase in recent years; an integral part of that phase is the emphasis on guides and how they can help people, who are still in the second stage of evolutionary growth, to release themselves from the effects of their use of free will, without, at the same time, interfering with their free will. The fundamental starting point is that people should accept their divinity, their unity with God, and that the acceptance should not just be intellectual but should also be in their feelings. It's not a question of doing anything, as such; it's simply letting a feeling happen, or letting go into a feeling. As the feeling of unity becomes a way of life, a person automatically fulfills his purpose as inevitably as a wave in the sea fulfills its purpose; there's no resistance to the flow (of life). For somebody who is aware enough to come to both an intellectual and a feeling acceptance of his divinity, it is likely, and more probably certain, that his purpose is to free himself completely from the wheel of karmic obligation, so that life on Earth will have no more to offer him by way of learning experiences. (It will, of course, be open to him to choose to reincarnate in order to help others.)

A source of huge confusion for people on Earth is that their conditioning links them to making judgments—including judgments on themselves, on happenings, or events. I know I'm repeating myself when I say that happenings are of no importance in themselves; their importance lies in the effects that they create on people's feelings and thoughts. The happenings are over and done with (and are succeeded by other happenings) but their effects remain; and the extent of the effects depends on the sensitivity of the people experiencing them. (The same thing can happen to two different people, but the effects on them will not be similar.)

The whole structure and functioning of planet Earth is based on happenings, on things being done. In spirit, creation is instantaneous; a soul in spirit has only to feel and think about something and it is. Whereas on Earth, feeling and thinking about something are not enough, although they are still the primary ingredients in creativity; something has to be done before there's a physical reality. It is understandable, then, that judgments are made on the basis of what people do rather than on what they feel or think. But it hardly requires deep consideration to see how artificial such judgments can be. Things are done for a multiplicity of reasons, some of which may be totally true to the feelings and thoughts behind them, but many of which are likely to be controlled by conditioned responses where the thoughts are in conflict with, and suppressing, the feelings. Nobody can validly make a judgment on the actions of another because no soul can enter another soul or know that soul's inner motivation.

In order, then, to be able to flow with life, to be more truly divine, a person needs to free himself from conditioning so that he can find purity in his motivation and not allow himself to be controlled by any judgmental thinking. His motivation is geared totally towards being himself, knowing that the more he can succeed in that aim, the more he will relate to his world, and the people in it, with an integrity of purpose. Embarking on that journey may be a source of revolution for him. He can no longer hide behind a mask of any kind. It's a difficult, often monumental, task to break away from many centuries of conditioning which has created its own form of security, and resists, with great intensity, every step of the process of being let go.

I seem to have digressed somewhat from talking specifically about marriage into discussing conditioning in general. Marriage, though, is the most central vehicle of conditioning on planet Earth. In saying earlier that to be more truly divine a person needs to free himself from conditioning, I don't want to be understood as implying that marriage as an institution has no place in the grand design. I mentioned that in itself it has no special spiritual significance; but it serves to bring two people together into a relationship which provides them with an opportunity to come to terms with intimacy, with being more truly themselves. If they are not controlled by conditioning, for example, what they think is expected of them, and if they can expand into an awareness, including a feeling, of their own divinity, partners in a marriage can be helped significantly in breaking the cycle of karmic obligation, although in the process they may temporarily find themselves in conflict with each other as well as with the institutional demands of the society in which they live. Ultimately, the object is that all relationships should be clear, i.e., not controlled by any strings, such as duty, possessiveness, human respect, pride, security, and that all people should relate to each other in an unconditionally loving way.

Those souls who are now on Earth and those who will be coming into Earth from now on are being given greater opportunities than have ever before been present in the evolution of Earth to free themselves from the reincarnational cycle. It's a difficult task. However, there's no limit to the help available. All that's needed is not to be too proud to ask for it and to be willing to receive it.

Special Relationships

I'd like to consider how individuality fits in with oneness, or nonseparation, and to expand our exploration into how, or whether, special relationships are consistent with oneness. By oneness I mean, of course, oneness with God/love/feeling and all its expressions.

The fundamental starting point in our consideration has to be that nothing exists outside of God; all is God, God is all, whatever way one likes to put it. Accordingly, as God is in each one of us, we are all linked together in God. In that sense we are all one. How, then, is there individuality?

Suppose we take an example of cars. There are all sorts of designs of cars, with vast differences between them. Yet they all have one thing in common: they cannot run without a supply of energy.

The God within us is the supply of energy that animates us. It's an unfailing, unending source of supply no matter what transitional forms our evolutionary journeys involve.

The love that is God does not have to express itself in any particular pattern; it evolves in whatever way it wishes. Expression into individual parts was (is) inherent in that evolution. While all the individual parts are animated by God and are thus inextricably linked to each other, each part is, nonetheless, completely individualistic; literally, a universe in itself.

The more aware souls become, the more they express the love (God) that they are. It becomes easier to love unconditionally because it becomes easier to look behind the defensive masks with which souls seek to cloak their vulnerability. The lovableness of each soul becomes more readily apparent.

If the aware soul, then, loves every other soul, does a hungering for special relationships reflect a lack of awareness? No. Love is of its nature expansive. The more aware a soul is, the more it wishes to spread itself, to let its loving expression know no frontiers.

The expression of God into individual parts enabled special affinities between souls. The notion of God as an entity without a variety of individual expression is one of stagnation which is not consistent with evolving consciousness. The ultimate return to full awareness of souls still on that path will not result in a loss of individuality into a merging with a Source (God). (There wouldn't be much fun in a soul communicating indefinitely with itself.)

Full awareness means an unconditionally loving relationship with all souls (oversouls). Within that, there are special affinities which cover a wide range of souls. And, within the ambit of the special affinities, there are what are commonly called soul mates, wonderfully intimate relationships between two souls. Every soul (oversoul) has a soul mate. There comes a time, or times, when souls are ready, consciously, to meet their soul mates while they are both in human form. That is possible within the ultimate context of oneness, and when it happens, the love these individuals have for all others is enhanced by the unlimited nature of their love for each other.

Sex

In an earlier session, I discussed the relative positions of the spiritual and the material in the overall scheme of things. My conclusion was that the material is an aid to the spiritual and not to be regarded as separate from it.

Possibly the most central and confused area in this context is that of physical relations between the sexes. On the one hand, there's a widely held view that promiscuity in sexual matters is a barrier to growth in spirituality; and, there's a less widely held view that any indulgence at all in sexual activity is detrimental to spirituality. On the other hand, strong arguments are put forward for achieving freedom and/or spirituality through the release of the body from its sexual inhibitions.

The human body was blueprinted in male and female forms not alone for obvious reproductive reasons but also as a means of achieving growth in awareness through inter- and contrasting relationships. That there should be physical attraction between the sexes is an integral part of the blueprint.

Society, in particular western society, is ordered in such a way that a man and a woman are, generally speaking, expected to be exclusive in their behavior; for example, if married, they should neither desire (at least obviously!) nor have sexual relations with anybody except each other; if single, they are expected to be faithful to one person (at least at a time); if attached to a religious order which has a rule of celibacy, they are forbidden to indulge in any sexual activity. The difficulty, then, facing both sexes is that they have inbuilt natural urges which they must restrain if they are not to be ostracized or condemned in some way by society.

It is interesting to look at sexual mores in the context of the different stages of evolutionary growth as I have outlined them. At the first, non-human, stage the natural urges are followed with, for the most part, no exclusivity. At the second, human stage exclusivity enters and there is restraint on the natural urges. After the second stage there is no longer sex differentiation; the division into male and female has served its purpose.

Sexual relations at the first stage tend to be direct and uncomplicated although they are preceded by mating rituals in some instances. At the second stage a greater degree of sophistication is generally sought and physical demonstrations of affection and communication, such as hugging, kissing, touching, are practiced both as incidental to explicitly sexual relationships and to relationships between members of families and between friends and acquaintances. At the other stages, the physical element is no longer present, but love is demonstrated in nonexclusive, more continuous, stronger and more pleasurable ways than is possible at the second stage. The best description I can give is that there is a fusion of being. By that I don't mean that any soul loses its individuality, even momentarily. There is a totality of understanding and of oneness of communication and of feeling (being) which is all the more comprehensive because of the consciousness of individuality which remains ever-present. If I merge into you (on the assumption that that could happen, which it couldn't), communication between us is no longer possible. But if you and I can achieve a form of communication where the love that we are simply manifests itself towards each other, through our being, with total openness and awareness of what we are, without the necessity for any type of camouflage or ritual and without any possibility of misunderstanding of any kind, then that is a state of perfect harmony which is a source of the greatest possible sharing of pleasure for both of us.

The only reason for the existence of the physical is so that it will serve as a means of helping spirit beings raise their levels of awareness. Accordingly, if the physical is not used for spiritual purposes, there is a waste of opportunity for growth. Translated into sexual terms this means that it is likely that promiscuous behavior, in the sense of obsession with the performance of the sexual act whether with another or others, is more of a hindrance than a help towards awareness (which, of course, applies to all obsessions).

There are many ways of arriving at the same end (increased awareness), no one of them necessarily better than another. In sexual matters, as with all others, it is most important to respect absolutely the free will of each person and its need to have its own "space," and to be free of all obsessions.

Now, again drawing attention to the fact that there are many ways towards increased awareness and that my way is only one of those, I feel it incumbent on me to give my suggestions which I hope will be of help in this basic and complex area of human relations.

For a start, I would not recommend overindulgence in sexual activity; not because I see it in black and white terms of right and wrong, but because it leads to dependence and obsessiveness.

Neither would I recommend sexual activity at all for its own sake, for example, as a means of physical release; if a person uses it for that purpose he will find himself increasingly dependent on it. By and large, the exclusivity which obtains in sexual activity is spiritually helpful in that with time it compels a reappraisal of values, and physical expression becomes less significant; in other words, physical attraction is not of predominant or unbalanced importance. In eternal terms this is very important since the physical has no part to play after the second stage, and life on Earth is intended as a preparation for moving into the third stage and beyond it. I know that there is a common belief that frustration, with all sorts of attendant problems, results from nonindulgence in sexual activity. Of course, it is only the belief which causes the problems; all frustrations are products of the mind.

Just as I don't recommend sexual activity for its own sake, neither do I recommend celibacy for its own sake. If undertaken as a means of mortifying the flesh, or if it is in any way perceived as a penance or a deprivation, it is likely to be detrimental to spiritual advancement.

Obsessiveness takes many forms. In sexual terms it can include fear of sexual expression as well as dependence on it. So, in one case, the solution from a spiritual point of view may lie in transforming this fear into love through, for example, a loving sexual relationship and, in the other, in reducing the level of sexual activity or, perhaps, becoming celibate, at least for a time.

So far I have outlined what I don't recommend. It's time for me to say what I do recommend. I think the clearest thing I can do is to list my recommendations and incidental comments, as follows:

1. If possible, study all sessions relating to God, feeling and emotion, freedom, free will, how the world came into being, the stages of evolutionary growth, reincarnation, the significance of the body within the spiritual continuity of life, and the mind (soul) with particular reference to the relationship between the mind and the body.

2. Having studied the sessions, you can now understand and accept, I hope, that life is a spiritual

reality; that physical life has no real meaning except in a spiritual context; that ultimately the only significance of the physical is as an aid or a vehicle for the spiritual and that there is no separation between them; and, finally, that the physical (matter) is entirely subject to the control of the spiritual (mind).

3. Consequently, if you concentrate on the physical or material in isolation from its spiritual importance you are separating yourself from yourself, in reality behaving unnaturally, and you will neither be able to find inner harmony nor make spiritual progress until you realize and accept this.

4. Physical demonstrations of love are not only desirable but necessary in certain relationships, for example, parents and children, but they are no substitute for true spiritual love which does not need to be physically expressed. Indeed, love which *demands* physical expression is likely to be emotion rather than feeling.

5. Ideally marital relationships, or similar types of relationships, should outgrow physical needs; in other words, sexual intercourse should be an experience of joyful spirituality which incorporates physical release to allow both partners to free themselves from any emotional obsessions, and to express themselves spiritually (i.e., fully) towards each other and towards all others with whom they come into contact.

6. In case of misunderstanding, I want to elaborate on what I have said at number four above, in order to make clear that I am not advocating abandonment, during a physical lifetime, of physical demonstrations of love. What I am trying to get

across is that such demonstrations cannot, of themselves, provide spiritual freedom. This can only be achieved when feeling replaces emotion. Feeling is a matter of being, not demonstration, and lack of demonstration does not necessarily imply aware or unaware expression of feeling; on the other hand, shows of demonstration do not necessarily imply aware or unaware expression of feeling, either. How feeling manifests itself is entirely an individual matter. However, I must add that, since the physical is an aid to the spiritual, it is a wonderful bonus when the body can be freely (i.e., nonobsessively) used in loving relationship, which of course includes sexual relationship.

7. In its ultimate state of awareness the soul is complete in itself and does not need anything. At the same time, it is one with all other souls and relates to them in total harmony of communication. The communication has a different form of expression geared to each soul, with each soul automatically knowing how to communicate with each other soul without any invasion of "space" by an unwelcome intrusion.

8. Whatever road you choose to travel on your way back to full awareness, you need to bear in mind that you cannot get back to that state without freeing yourself completely from even the minutest form of obsession. Obviously, it is a great step forward if you can succeed in doing this to a significant extent while still surrounded by powerful sources of obsession, as happens on Earth, which is what makes life on Earth such a marvelous learning experience.

9. Joy is a central attribute of spirit, so ideally, life on Earth and all its physical accompaniments and

arrangements should be a source of joy. The physical circumstances which give rise to joy change or are differently perceived as awareness increases; difficulties may occur in relationships if this is not understood. Ultimately, each person must come to terms with the fact that his brief stay on Earth is an opportunity which he has chosen primarily for his own spiritual growth; not anybody else's. Of course, if he can help others to grow too, that's great and, the more he grows, the more he can help.

Politics

On the face of it, it may be somewhat surprising that I should consider politics as a subject for discussion. I think it desirable that I do so since the business of politics affects the day-to-day living of people to a significant extent in one way or another.

In the modern world the process of government has largely evolved from imperial and monarchical systems to democracies of various kinds. The transition has been from government by acquisition or inheritance to election or selection from amongst the people themselves. Imperial and monarchical systems recognized and, indeed, promoted inequalities, for instance, through the establishment of different classes of nobility. In a democracy all the people have equal rights (in theory, at least).

As you would expect, the evolution of governmental systems is in accordance with the grand design and shows that, in spite of all the pronouncements and apparent indications to the contrary (including two world wars in the twentieth century), much progress has been made in the implementation of the design. In human terms, the emphasis on the value of the individual and respect for the individual has never been greater than it is today.

The movement towards democracy is, in fact, a reflection of the movement towards the seventh and ultimate stage of awareness. The seventh stage is an ideal form of democracy. Whereas in the human condition there are governments and laws and people placed in positions of authority over others, which to some extent negates the idea of equality, at the seventh stage there is absolute equality and there is no need for any of these restrictions.

Politics, in the democratic sense, has come to be regarded as an activity in which people engage in order to get themselves or others elected as public representatives, and, thus, into a position to regulate the business of government. There are, of course, different levels of engagement in politics. At the lowest or minimum level are the people whose activity is confined to voting in elections. Then there are those who seek the assistance of public representatives either for personal or community purposes. There are the people behind the scenes, the backroom workers, the canvassers of votes, the financial supporters, who stay out of the limelight themselves, but who do all in their power to get particular persons or parties elected to representative office. There are the people who seek, or allow themselves to be selected for, representative positions. And ultimately there are the people who become the leaders or the government.

The democratic system in its human context provides many learning opportunities from a spiritual point of view. The person who is obsessed with power gets much scope to free himself from his obsession; so does the person who craves for recognition; as does the person who thinks he knows what's best for others; or the person who needs to be occupied all the time; or the person who hates being alone;

or the person who is driven by missionary fervor in the service of others.

As a person becomes more aware, he will find himself less inclined to become involved in political activity. He will see that the management of people's affairs is primarily a matter for themselves and that it is their right to be allowed to develop in their own way which doesn't preclude their being helped, if they so wish. A person who is actively involved in politics is continually seeking to impress on others his point of view or the point of view of his party. His actions in favor of one person may well obstruct another's opportunity.

But, you object, somebody has to run a country or a community; somebody has to make laws and see that they are observed, otherwise there will be chaos. Yes, unfortunately, that is still the position. While it remains so, and it will until each person has total respect for the free will of all others and has absolute tolerance of them and acceptance of their equality in God with him, the Earth experiment, or something similar, will continue to be needed.

Well, then, as a person gains awareness, how does he live with the system as it is? By keeping himself free, as far as he can, in his feelings and thoughts; by sharing those feelings and thoughts, without in any way seeking to impose them on others when suitable opportunities to do so occur; and by helping in that way to create more accepting and tolerant communities in which souls will have freedom to expand their consciousness. A restricted, narrow-minded community is like a garden where the flowers are stunted by weeds and thorn bushes; whereas a liberal, open-minded community is like a garden where the flowers bloom in the sun with nothing to inhibit their growth.

Does the practice of politics not give a ready made, and in many ways an ideal, platform for the sharing of feelings and thoughts? In my view, no. Politics is a competitive business. One politician is successful only at the expense of another. He is concerned with establishing that his thoughts and actions are superior to those of another or others. It is difficult for him to be sincere with himself or with others. He is, in practice, at all times making a plea for recognition, and if his plea is not successful he doesn't get elected to representative office. To the aware person recognition doesn't count. He manifests himself as he is; how others react to him is exclusively their affair.

While politicians give public expression to a craving for recognition, such craving is common, in varying degrees, to human beings generally. Politics and politicians play their own part in the grand design in a more public and dramatic way than most others. Politicians as a group are likely to be neither more nor less aware than the majority of the people whom they represent; they are, in fact, likely to mirror the state of awareness of the community which they represent.

One final thought; there's a big difference between sharing your thoughts with others and seeking to influence others to your way of thinking. I might have said that there was all the difference in the world, but it would be more accurate to say that there's a world of awareness in the difference.

Activity

Activity of one kind or another is common to all souls. It is not possible to "be" and not be active. The soul is in fact always active even when it is using a physical body and even when that body is asleep.

The soul is feeling and feeling is active; it is eternally creative by thought, word, and deed. Paradoxically, its greatest creativity is likely to be when the body is still or apparently passive.

In this session I intend the word "activity" to include work in the sense in which I think work is commonly understood, that which people do in order to earn money or keep house so that they can provide the necessities and luxuries of physical living for themselves and their families.

By and large, work is generally perceived to be a form of slavery. It is exceptional for people to find jobs which give them satisfaction on a continuing basis. Yet workplaces provide other forms of satisfaction; for example, companionship, a sense of belonging, a feeling of compatibility with others, status, fulfillment of ambition.

In modern times technology, particularly computers, is taking over much of the work previously performed manually. This is making life easier, on the one hand, but is increasing unemployment on the other. Many people are now coming on the job market whose prospects of ever getting continuous employment or even any employment at all are slim. So, since a reversion to pre-computer practices is unlikely, people are faced with a double challenge of accepting a lower standard of living and of arriving at a new perception of work and of leisure which will have the effect of making both more enjoyable and productive.

You may remember that spiritually no particular activity has, of itself, greater value than another. An activity acquires value from its effect on the person who performs it. One man will get great value from a particular type of work, whereas another will find it boring and frustrating. One person will get agitated and suffer sleepless nights over work problems; another will take similar problems in his stride and see them as challenges to be faced and enjoyed.

A common example of frustration is that of a person who is employed in what to him seems to be a dull, routine job and who feels that he has missed out, or is missing out, on opportunities to do something meaningful with his life.

Here again the separation between the spiritual and material becomes apparent; for instance, charitable or missionary activity assumes an aura of importance which is not perceived in a routine clerical job.

Unfortunately, I can't wave a magic wand and take the slavery out of work although I have tried to show ways of doing this in the session on freedom. If people can accept that before they were born they chose the environment and the work most suited to the achievement of their particular life purpose, it should be easier for them to reconcile themselves to their jobs and to begin to look on them in a different light, and, hopefully, to see that their only missed opportunity is in their attitude to their jobs.

This is a subject which is of more than passing interest to you personally. You work at a job and in your spare time you do what might be loosely described as counseling. From the spiritual point of view you see your voluntary activity as being the much more important and you would wish to be in a position, financially, to do it full-time.

Two questions arise: is, in fact, your work as important for you spiritually as your voluntary activity; and how can the only importance, spiritually, of your voluntary activity lie in its effect on yourself?

Now I have to remind you that you chose your work. There were certain lessons which you wanted to learn in this lifetime and which you could best learn in the type of work and environment in which you operate. Once you have learned these lessons it will no longer be necessary for you to continue with that work. So the answer to your first question is that at the present time your work is just as important for you spiritually as your voluntary activity. In fact, one complements the other in helping you fulfill your life purpose.

You can readily appreciate the effect of these sessions on yourself. But how can that be their only importance spiritually? Surely by encouraging you to write down all this material I am assigning importance to the material, not just for you but for others. It is certainly my hope and the hope of the others who have joined with me on this project that many people will read and be helped by your record of our sessions. But the reading of it becomes their activity; and for them the only importance, spiritually, of that reading will be its effect on themselves. If what you are writing now is never published or nobody but yourself ever reads it, you can see that your activity in receiving and writing it can have no importance spiritually except in its effect on you. If it is published, people will have to decide for themselves whether to read it or not; that is their effort, their activity, and the effect of the reading will be different for each individual.

You are still not satisfied. You argue that if a book is read by say, a million people and most of them are helped in some way by it, doesn't that make the book important in itself? You forget I was talking about activity. The book is a product of activity and it is an instrument of activity for as long as it is being read; but it just lies there until somebody chooses to read it, and then the effect it produces is entirely a matter for that person. In itself a book has whatever importance a person or people assign to it.

Now, you see, I have made a distinction between the fruit of a person's activity, for example, a book, and the activity itself, for example, the writing of a book. The actual outcome of the writing (the book) has relative importance for each of its readers and is important in itself for that reason; but its readers' activity in reading it is of importance, spiritually, only in its effect on themselves.

All this may sound rather abstruse so perhaps two illustrations may help.

A man works for most of his life in a routine, apparently unimportant, job. He's a cheerful, happy man, who brings his disposition to bear on his job and the whole environment in which he lives and works.

Another man is a highly successful writer. His books are generally acknowledged to be opinion-shapers towards a liberalization of attitudes. Yet he himself is discontented with the pace of change, and he manifests that discontent in the environment in which he operates.

Objectively, it is probably true that the body of work which the second man has created has more accrued importance than that of the first. Yet it is also probably true that from a spiritual point of view the first man has gained more from his activity than the second man.

In both cases the only importance of their activities lies in their effects on themselves. The results of their activities may have relative importance for other people, but again, the scale of that importance is determined by their own activities in responding to those results.

It would be a useful exercise for a person to list the lessons or the learning experiences which he feels his work has offered him from a spiritual point of view, and then to evaluate his response to those lessons or experiences.

Money

I think that nobody will dispute that money occupies a central place in most people's thoughts. People have to find money every day for basic necessities; food, shelter, etc. Some people, a minority, don't have to concern themselves about money in the sense of not having enough to meet day-to-day needs; but they are likely to be involved in financial activities, such as speculating on the stock market, studying investment possibilities, considering business opportunities, funding payrolls, buying and selling in some form. No matter what people do, whether it's going to a supermarket, or a shop, or a public house, or a hairdresser, or a cinema, or a football match, or indeed almost anywhere one can imagine, unless it's just for a walk, they need money. People worry themselves sick over money, burden themselves with heavy debts, rob each other, sometimes even kill each other; they play lotteries, and they fantasize about winning big amounts of money. Those who can get paid employment spend a major part of their lives working, often in unsatisfying jobs, for meager, yet necessary, incomes. People can't even die respectably without leaving money behind them for the disposal of their bodily remains. And I need hardly comment on how much energy is centered on wills or the lack of them.

One of the biggest problem areas where money is concerned is in what tends to be seen as a conflict between the spiritual and physical or material worlds. I'm assuming that people who don't believe in life beyond what they experience on Earth don't have any difficulties around the concept of money; the *concept,* as distinct from the actuality of whether they have enough money for their needs or fantasies. Accordingly, I'm addressing myself to those who believe that people are a continuity of spirit, that when they are finished with their bodies they move on to another dimension of existence.

As you know, it's part of the culture that has evolved through the ages around the expression of spirituality that that expression involves rejection of the physical or material. But, if people are spiritual beings, souls with bodies rather than bodies with souls, and if they accept that they continue to exist as souls, why are they on Earth at all? Surely it must be in order to experience whatever Earth has to offer so that they can learn from that experience and grow in awareness or consciousness? And, since money plays such a central role in the Earth experience, they, as souls, must have something valuable to learn from how to deal with it. In my view, if people go through life without learning how to deal with money they will have missed out on an important opportunity for growth in spiritual awareness.

The purpose of life on Earth for people is, fundamentally and essentially, to free themselves from a feeling of separation into a feeling of unity or oneness. This cannot be said too often. At the root of their feeling of separation is their concept of God. If they put God into a mold separate from themselves they are placing a limit on themselves as well as, of course, on God; and, in that limitation, they are separating themselves from themselves. But once they can accept that all life, everything including themselves, is contained in God, they know that there's no separation between the worlds of spirit and Earth; that all is spirit, that Earth operates as an aid to the spiritual, that the energy of God/love infuses all creation and creation inevitably, ineluctably, includes money as things are, at present, organized on Earth.

It is clear then that people as individuals actually own nothing on Earth. They have a loan of things; their bodies, whatever they use, including, of course, money. All the things of Earth are part of a flowing cycle of energy, going in, out, round and round. Money is an expression of energy. People need it to survive on Earth like they need air or water, but, just as they don't own air or water, they don't own money. If they become obsessive about owning money as, indeed, about any form of ownership, including possessiveness of spouses, lovers, children, they block the flow of energy and place severe limitations on their growth in consciousness. When they accept and feel themselves in union with God they have freedom to give and receive, to let all the energy of the universe work through them, for them, in them, helping themselves and all others. Their guides, of course, help them towards that union and, in the process, to expand more and more into their higher selves or oversouls.

If you don't own any money how can you pay your bills? You don't own your bills either, although you often tend to act as if you do; you curse them, worry about them, resist them. I suggest that you try to let go of all resistance to them and to see them as part of the flow of energy. It may take a while for you to reach the stage of giving whoops of delight when bills find you. But it will get easier. I suggest that you remind yourself that paying your bills is a form of giving; and, in not resisting giving, it will be easier for you not to resist receiving, either. Bear in mind that it's all expression of divine energy and that you're privileged and entitled to share in that expression. Knowing that the flow of divine energy never falters and can never falter, you can let yourself trust in the infinite supply of that energy, and even say "thanks" for the opportunity to pay yet another bill!

How To Become More Clairvoyant/Clairaudient

How can one become more clairvoyant or clairaudient; in other words, break down the barriers between what are classified as the natural and supernatural? We have looked at this earlier in talking about communication with guides. I'd like to go into the subject in more detail in this session.

The following are my suggestions:

1. Ask for guidance.
2. Get yourself into as relaxed a position as possible by whatever method suits you.
3. Let yourself go mentally limp; in other words, suspend thought as far as you can.

4. Press, briefly and occasionally, your right thumb into your throat just below the comer of your jaw. This is an aid towards clairaudience.

5. Massage, slowly and gently, again with your right thumb, the third eye area in the middle of the forehead in an counterclockwise direction for about two to three minutes a day. This helps clairvoyance.

6. Bear in mind that communication is a continuing process and that one doesn't have to wait for "a flash of lightning"; once you consciously tune in, the insights that come to you are likely to be valuable.

7. Don't let yourself be pressurized by the passage of time; silence may be exactly what's needed in a particular situation, so if you have a blank, don't worry about it.

8. Communication is easier if you have specific questions as long as you free yourself from commitment to a particular answer (which might be likely to confuse your communication).

9. Don't seek to give directions or to control. Aware guidance is always given in a nondirective way so that free will is never imposed upon. The central purpose of this type of communication is to increase awareness, not to encourage the generation of robots.

10. Don't make any judgments. Remember that there are no absolutes. Judging is an ego trip and is likely to follow the pattern of your own conditioning.

11. Bear in mind that communication between the nonphysical and physical worlds is normal rather than abnormal, but that there are difficulties

related to time and space which are a feature of Earth life only; so don't adopt black and white standards or take too literally what you're given.

12. Trust your imagination, especially when you're in a relaxed frame of mind. Once you have asked your guides not to let negative influences come through to you, your imagination will provide the answers you need.

13. Good communication is not a matter of technique but rather of relaxation, patience, trust, commitment, honesty, open-mindedness, tolerance, freedom from conditioning, respect for each soul's privacy and free will, and, above all, expanding love.

Communication with guides is not designed to be straightforward in the sense of the guides doing all the work; otherwise there would be little or no growth for the human communicator. Ideally, as communication develops, it is difficult to distinguish between what's coming from guides and what's in the mind of the human agent; the human and non-human (spirit) merge in an integrity of communication. Thus the human is never just a channel. All his previous experience, through countless centuries in terms of Earth time, has brought him to a level of awareness which he now shares with others, while at the same time he leaves himself open to inspiration which is flowing to him from his spiritual helpers. All through history the people who have helped to raise awareness have been able to do so because they consciously or unconsciously left themselves open to inspiration. That in no way diminishes them; rather the reverse, since they reached out beyond the limits of the physical framework to tap into the universal consciousness. Even though we are, each, individual, yet we are all one, so that my contribution to the universal consciousness is equally yours as yours is mine. That's why it is so important that each soul finds its way back to full awareness; in doing so, it automatically helps every other soul.

How to Release Your Creative Potential

Everybody, without exception, is creative, but the trouble is that most human beings either aren't aware of their own creative potential or don't get a chance to express it.

What constitutes creativity? The birth of a baby, certainly. Suppose somebody writes a book that no publisher will accept for publication, or paints a picture that nobody will buy, or composes music that nobody considers worth playing, or designs a building that by general consensus is an eyesore, and so on. Is that creativity? Is creativity insofar as literature, art, etc., are concerned to be measured by critical acceptance of them?

In my view, creativity can't be defined by any popular perception of it. It has a multitude of forms, apart from the obvious procreative one, such as, writing a poem, a play, a short story, a book, a letter, painting a picture, a wall, sculpting, designing a bridge, a building, planting a flower, a tree, making love, a cake, a dress, composing a song, a symphony, playing a musical instrument, singing, acting, direction (of plays, movies), photography, filming, storytelling, dancing, sport, computer programming, mechanical inventiveness, embroidery, tapestry, carpentry, flower arranging, hairdressing, farming. In fact, however a person is, or whatever he does, is creative in some form. Each person will perform the most routine procedures in his own style which is peculiar to him alone.

In this session, then, when I'm talking about releasing creative potential what I mean is finding fulfillment.

In utopia everybody will be fulfilled. Unfortunately, however, realization of utopia, while initially attainable for some people in a relatively short period of time, will extend throughout the planet in stages of seemingly tortoiselike progression. I convey this image with all the optimism related to the legendary endurance of the tortoise in reaching its goal.

Most people on the planet will, for many years ahead, have to exist in an interim situation where they must conform to restrictive systems and spend much of their waking time performing work which they wouldn't choose to do if they didn't have to provide an income for themselves and their dependents, if any, or in being unable to find remunerative employment at all. How are they going to find fulfillment?

I'd like to suggest ways by which greater degrees of fulfillment can be achieved, no matter how restrictive you may consider your present situation to be.

1. Do you believe that life on Earth is intended to be a penitential, self-sacrificing, journey, which, if endured patiently, will lead to eternal reward in heaven? Or do you believe that it's okay to be happy while you're on Earth, or that you deserve to be happy? If the former, you're in a mindset which finds fulfillment (if that's the appropriate word!) readily to hand in existing conditions on Earth. At this stage my words will have relevance only for those who subscribe to the latter belief, and my hope is that more and more people will shift from the first category to the second.

2. As your life has evolved you'll have found that you enjoy some activities more than others. Make a list of what you enjoy. How much do those items feature in your day-to-day life? Do any of them

manifest in your present work? If you are unemployed, are any of them relevant to your present lifestyle?

3. Apart from what you have found that you enjoy, what dreams did you have as a child, or as you grew into adulthood, of what you would like to be or do? Please add those dreams, if any, to your list. What stopped you from realizing them? What would it take to make them a reality? Would you, in fact, want them to materialize for you now if you had the means to make that happen?

4. As you proceed with your exploration, you will notice how your creativity has been continually expressing itself even though you were probably not at all aware of it. For example, your taste in reading, movies, theater, sport, hobbies, conversation, friends, will be likely to have been subject to wide variation through your life so far. Imperceptibly, you are constantly evolving, and the you that you are expressing today is different in some degree from the you of yesterday.

5. Accordingly, in making your lists it's important to bear in mind that what you enjoy doing today you may not enjoy tomorrow. People may feel frustrated in their present existence because they see no opportunity to follow their dreams. But how often has it transpired that, for those who at some stage found such opportunities, the reality turned out to be totally disappointing?

6. Ideally, what you want is that you will be able to live your life in a continuing enjoyment of every moment, accepting that you have only the present moment, since you can't live in the past or the future, and bearing in mind that sources of

enjoyment for you may be subject to constant or periodic change. Is there any point, then, you may well ask, in making lists, as I have suggested, of what you enjoy at present, and/or your dreams? The reason why I have suggested making the lists is that by doing so you are focusing your energy and looking at how you're living your life. If, for example, you see yourself as being trapped in a continuing round of duties, responsibilities, financial pressures, relationship problems, non-stimulating work, and so on, you are locked into a negative pattern of energy which is self-perpetuating. Understandably, you might say that it's easy for me in my celestial smugness to expound simplistic diagnoses, but you are stuck with coping with the physical realities as they are.

7. No matter how much you may seem to be a victim of circumstances, you still have the power to change your life. That power is within you; you can exercise it positively or negatively. One thing is certain, there will not be positive direction in your life unless you decide to make it so.

8. Once you make the decision that you want to express yourself in your living in a manner that will provide you with creative fulfillment, and at present you feel that you can find such fulfillment in the ways outlined in your lists, I suggest that you then hand over the lists to your guides, thereby aligning yourself with all the evolved energy of the universe (God) and enabling opportunities to manifest in line with your unfolding and, perhaps, changing perceptions of sources of enjoyment for you. In the handing over process you are accepting that you have set the wheels in motion for you to be supported by the infinite, universal energy

(God) through: exercising your own free will; giving positive direction to your energy by outlining how you'd like to express yourself, while understanding that you are doing this in accordance with your present perceptions of what you want, and allowing yourself flexibility to respond to your changing perceptions in the knowledge and trust that your guides are keeping a constant overview of your (soul) purpose; and, acknowledging that you need help.

9. When the time comes for you to say thanks to your body and leave it, and you look back on your physical journey, your review of it won't be concerned with how many possessions you acquired, what recognition you achieved, what status you earned, etc.; your only concern, ultimately, will be to what extent you were able to release and enjoy your creative potential; in other words, your divinity. My earnest wish is that the questions I have raised and the suggestions I have made will help you towards that end.

Criticism and How to Deal with It

I'm talking about criticism in its narrow meaning of finding fault, rather than as evaluation of, say, art, drama, literature; in other words, in its negative, rather than positive aspect.

Criticism is a great leveler. It is probably the biggest barrier of all to self-expression. It is all-pervasive in that it works both from the inside and the outside; the self-critic as well as the self-appointed one.

Criticism that comes from outside is of no importance in the long run, or, at most, it's only important if you allow it to affect you. Whether you are self-critical, or to the extent that you are, is all that matters.

Since people aren't born and don't live in isolation from each other, there's bound to be interaction between them. Physical existence, as you know it, is ordered in communities of continents, nation/states, indigenous arrangements, families. Usually, there are laws, customs and cultural mores which create expectations in general and specific ways as to how people should live their lives. Accordingly, it can seem to be a safe way for a person to get by if he doesn't draw attention to himself by being "different," unless the attention results from some achievement, or way of life, which is generally regarded as praiseworthy.

How did you become self-critical? Through a combination of circumstances. As a soul on a continuing journey towards regaining lost awareness, you will more than likely have experienced a number of physical lifetimes, effects from which you carried through into your present life. You chose to be born into an environment which would be likely to help you to deal with those effects, probably by facing you with them through your contact with people around you. For example, your parents are seen as respected members of the community; that's the public image of your family grouping. At home, however, there's a lot of tension, with no real communication between your parents. You, being very sensitive, are affected by the tension, without knowing its source. Perhaps, you think, you are the cause of it. One or both of your parents may be preoccupied and not available to listen to you or take notice of you; maybe there's something wrong with you that they're like that? What can you do to get their attention, their approval? You begin to watch yourself, to be self-conscious, to analyze people's reactions to you as you perceive them. Your inner critic is becoming well-established, nurtured, and blooming. At school, a teacher makes disparaging remarks about your efforts at art or music or writing and your creative expression is stunted; better to play safe and do something useful, functional, with your life; whatever you do, don't leave yourself open to being a target for somebody to downgrade or humiliate you!

You exist, then, on a superficial level without ever giving yourself a chance to explore your deeper, innermost, creativity. You will probably have convinced yourself that you're not at all creative, and so to a large extent you waste the potential which you provided for yourself in undertaking a physical transition.

That's just one scenario. Opportunities to develop and reinforce self-critical faculties are myriad. People in your life, from your parents onwards, are catalysts in one way or another. They all mirror you to yourself in how you relate to them. Your strength is determined by how free from control you are in your interaction with them.

If somebody is behaving in a critical manner towards you, what's happening? That person is seeing you, or aspects of you, from his perspective, his place in the jigsaw. He cannot be aware, no matter how well he thinks he knows you, of what's really going on inside you, your feelings, your thoughts, your inner motivation. The same thing applies, of course, if you are critical of another.

Once you accept, in both your feelings and thoughts, that nobody is in a position to tell you how to live your life, that, irrespective of whatever authority any person may arrogate to himself in expressing a judgment on you or your behavior, your life on Earth is your journey and only yours, you will be able to listen in a detached way to any criticism. If there are aspects of it that make sense to you, you'll be in a position to assess them objectively and respond to them constructively.

Ultimate security lies in accepting and feeling God in you, and in acknowledging that God is also in everybody else. Then you won't be inclined to find fault with anybody, including, of course, yourself.

How to Be Successful

A common source of pressure among human beings is to be accepted, and to accept themselves, as successes rather than failures. If that's so, it's reasonable to assume that there are general perceptions as to what constitutes success or failure. What are those perceptions?

Success is generally equated with, for example, material possessions, power, status, notable achievement, recognition of talent, fame, family security, sexual attractiveness, lovableness; while failure would encompass the lack of some or all of those.

When we consider how the spiritual and physical worlds can be increasingly integrated, perceptions of success and failure can bring us into diametrically opposed territories. It is, I suppose, obvious that somebody who amasses a considerable fortune through, say, entrepreneurial abilities may achieve widespread recognition on that account; but, when he comes to the end of his physical life, may find that he hasn't advanced, or may even have regressed, in spiritual terms. A person who lives a life of total obscurity may achieve far greater spiritual growth than one who becomes a celebrity, but the reverse may also be so. Choosing to reject participation in the world of commerce may be no greater guarantee of spiritual growth than opting to immerse oneself in that world.

The question posed in this session is how to be successful. Implicit in that question is, of course, success in spiritual terms. Any reader who has been with us so far would, I'm sure, find any other interpretation somewhat surprising.

Because all human endeavor is expressed in stages and in a linear way, since you live within a time structure, it will be helpful, I hope, to set out, as follows, ingredients which, in my view, are essential towards the achievement of success.

Open-mindedness and tolerance:

All human beings, without exception, are limited in their thinking by environmental, cultural, religious, and ancestral influences. It is most important to acknowledge that, so that you no longer restrict yourself by taking up immediate and often fixed positions, which are inevitably controlled by your own experience. This doesn't mean that you stop yourself from expressing opinions; what it does mean is that you allow that your opinions are just your way, for the present, of looking at whatever comes within the ambit of your day-to-day existence. It also means that you accept without reservation the validity, from their point of view, of all others' ways of expression, and that you do not attempt to manipulate or control how they express themselves. This doesn't imply that you won't help people, as best you can, to find their way; rather you will always allow them, unreservedly, freedom of choice.

Flexibility:

In your day-to-day life you have, of course, to organize and plan; for example, the clothes you're going to wear, what you're going to eat, how you're going to allocate your time. Because you live in a physical world you have no choice, no matter how nonconformist you may be, but to deal with structures of time and space and the society in which you happen to be. It is understandable, then, that you may settle into fixed patterns of thinking and behavior, and that any change in that pattern is disturbing for you. But the way of spirit is ever fluid, so that, if your life on Earth is to fulfill its purpose, you need to be able to flow freely with change. If you're not flexible, you'll find, inevitably, that you're going to be faced with changes on a recurring basis until you reach a level of adaptability.

Creativity:

Everybody, without exception, is creative, but most people don't believe that they are, and have never found ways of expressing their full creative potential. That's understandable because so many people are on the edge of survival struggling to have the minimal necessities, such as food and shelter, for the continuation of physical life. But yet it is true that the way people feel and think sets up a vibration which affects positively or negatively the conditions under which they live. In spiritual terms creativity means how souls feel and think. For a soul in spirit that's very obvious because the results are immediate. But the human being caught in a linear time frame and physical structure needs patience to see the effects of how he feels and thinks.

For example, a soul in spirit wishes to have a particular type of house and the house manifests immediately without any prohibitive, financial, complications. But for the human the wish is only the beginning of a long and detailed process until the house becomes a reality. Partners in a relationship, say, are likely to be faced with a heavy mortgage repayable over a lengthy period of time. Suppose they find themselves in a situation where they have been unable to pay the mortgage debt and are threatened with repossession of the family home, which will have the effect of leaving them and their children homeless. In their view, no amount of creative thinking, for example, imagining the manifestation of the money needed to solve their problem, will change the dire situation they're in. So, as time goes on, they are more and more locked into a negative way of being where they will always be victims of circumstances, which, they feel, are outside of their control. Yet it is undoubtedly a fact that, even though on the face of it their situation is totally restrictive, the power to change it positively lies within themselves, in how they feel and think. Once they accept that they are continually creating their own destiny and take total responsibility for themselves, solutions will always present themselves; it's the constant, undeviating, way of the universe. It cannot be otherwise.

Truth:

What I mean is being true to yourself. No matter how you try, you cannot relate to any two people in the same way; for each of them there will be shades of difference in your appearance, in what you say, in what you do, in how you are, even in your silences. So there's no point in trying to establish an image of how you think you ought to be, or how you think a person, or people generally, expect you to be. The statement to the effect that nobody can serve God and Mammon has, in my view, generally been completely misinterpreted; what it means is that nobody can be at one with God in him, and, at the same time, serve a self-imposed image of what he thinks is expected of him by another and/or others. It is an essential ingredient in success that you present yourself to the world as you really are and let the world react in whatever way it will. That's not easy, but, if you're patient and tolerant with yourself, it will eventually become easier.

Being true to yourself doesn't mean that you have to reveal your all to everybody in your life or to make your views known at every available opportunity. It simply means that you're free to be whatever way you want to be, in how you are in yourself, how you feel and think, while, of course, always respecting others' truths.

Letting go:

It is, of course, implicit in being true to yourself that you let go of egotism, i.e., the fearful, insecure, little "i." When I talk about letting go, I don't mean letting go of, or out of but, rather, letting go into, i.e., into the greater "I," the divine "I." How can you do that? By accepting that you are divine, that you are in God and God is in you; also accepting that, as you are at present manifesting, you are revealing only an aspect of you as oversoul; and aligning yourself (ideally, in conscious cooperation with your guides) with your own divinity, with God in you and with God in all there is.

A central question in all this is, how can you align yourself with something you don't know? All your conditioning prepares you to move from the known to the known, so that you will invariably make a judgment on the basis of your own experience or knowledge as to how you will proceed in any given situation. Security for you tends to lie in being able to make an analysis fit into the box of your understanding and, of course, all boxes are structured and defined and limited. So, you're at a loss, operating within limitation, when you consider God. You cannot limit God, analyze God, or *know* God, so it is impossible for you to align yourself with God through your thinking, analytical processes. You need to go beyond thought. Where does that lead you? All that's beyond thought is feeling. You can feel God in all sorts of ways (such as those we have outlined in the session on imagination), but, ultimately, in how you love. Once you love unconditionally, you are one with your own divinity and with God in you and in all. You are then unlimited because you set no limits, and you have truly let go *into* rather than *out* of.

How do you know whether you're living successfully?

You may say that it's easy to talk about unconditional love in an abstract or theoretical way, but what does it mean in practice? A useful test, I suggest, would be to ask yourself a number of questions, such as the following:

-How much of your energy is expended on worry (for example, about money, family, work, relationships)?

Your rate of success is diminished to the extent that you worry at all. (Understandably, you may feel that it's asking the impossible of any human being not to worry; but it's a habit which you can break, for example, by handing things over to your guides.)

-How possessive are you (for example, of spouse, lover, children, material things)?

Successful living is always limited by possessiveness.

-How tolerant are you of all others (for example, their views, behavior)?

Successful living doesn't allow for any exceptions; that doesn't mean, of course, that you have to agree with everybody.

-How jealous/envious are you of others (for example, their possessions, looks, fame, lovers)?

Not at all, ideally.

-Do you hate, resent, or feel angry towards, another/others on a continuing basis?

Allow for your humanity, in occasional bursts!

-How much are you controlled by a need to project a certain image of yourself (for example, your perception of how you wish another/others to see you)?

Again, ideally, not at all.

-How sincere are you in your relationship with others?

Not an easy question; the simplest way to approach it, I suggest, is to use a barometer of how you would wish others to relate to you.

-How respectful are you of others' space, privacy, free will?

A central difficulty with this question is how to distinguish between helpfulness and interference; helpfulness is exploration of potential and choices in nondirective ways and is always geared towards increasing awareness (for example, how guides/guardian angels operate). Interference is controlling and arrogant in its assumption that one knows what's best for another.

-How comfortable are you with yourself? (For example, do you impose a burden of perfection according to your own perception, inevitably on yourself? Do you regularly observe yourself in a self-critical way? Is it difficult for you to be alone for an extended period? Are you dependent on other people to provide you with entertainment, fulfillment, etc.?)

The more you enjoy your own company and/or the company of others without feeling pressure either to be continually with others or continually by yourself, and, of course, the more you accept yourself as you are, the more successful you are.

-How addictive are you (for example, to drugs, alcohol, food, sports, sex, television)?

Anything that's a controlling factor in your life, in other words, when you feel you can't manage without it, restricts your success; the free spirit enjoys, without being controlled.

-Do you feel stressed or under pressure in any area (for example, work, sex, relationship, health)?

It's very difficult, if not impossible, to be human and not to feel stressed or under pressure at some times; if the feeling is more constant than random, it's time for remedial action.

141

-How open-minded are you in your views and beliefs (as distinct from being tolerant of others)?

It's equally important, from a success point of view, that you're as tolerant and open-minded with yourself as you are with others; rigidly held beliefs (for example, religious, political, atheistic) are inescapably limiting.

-How fulfilled do you feel in your creativity?

Creation of masterpieces in art, literature, etc., is not a prerequisite for fulfillment. The real criterion, I suggest, is how much you enjoy yourself in how you are and whatever you do.

-Do you accept and feel your oneness with God?

This is the ultimate question which contains all the others. How you live your life determines how much you are at one with God. An atheist could be more in union with God than an ardent believer (although I don't suppose either of them would be too pleased to hear that).

While all souls are uniquely individual, they are each part of God (love). While an atheist may well live his life to a large extent in unconscious unity with God, he consciously separates himself from God. But so, too, does the person who, because of his beliefs—usually religious—sees God as a separate entity.

Conscious acceptance of oneness with God, of God in you, is so important because then you can align yourself with all the infinite love that is God, thus allowing yourself the opportunities for complete fulfillment in your life.

You don't need to employ any elaborate rituals in order to align yourself more consciously with God. The love that is God is already in you, so all that's needed is to release that love more and more unconditionally to yourself and to all others.

Part III

Further Exploration in the Light of Evolving Consciousness of the Boundaries of Communication between the Spirit and Physical Worlds

As people have moved in their evolution from the instinctual animal to the rational human state they generally seem to think that value accrues with complexity. In spite of unprecedented advances in technology, it appears that business can't be conducted without being controlled by all sorts of laws, rules, and regulations involving increasingly diverse specialties, such as law, accountancy, taxation. The same thing applies to other areas, such as medicine, religion, legal structures, public institutions; can you think of any exception?

As has been the case in what would tend to be seen as the material world, so, also, complexity has been a feature of people's perception of spiritual echelons, ranging from God to hierarchies of archangels, angels, saints, illuminated Masters, and so on, through multiple levels of perceived holiness or spiritual attainment.

From where I sit there's no complexity, just utter simplicity. Every soul is divine, a part of God. Some souls, a small minority, lost their awareness of themselves and have been struggling to regain it. Accordingly, there is a transitional period during which there are differing levels of awareness. Ultimately there will be no distinctions; all will be equal, yet uniquely individual, in their regained awareness of their divinity.

In the meantime you are experiencing humanity with all its density while, at the same time, conscious that you are a spirit being temporarily using a physical body. The challenge for you is how to integrate, as far as possible, the material and spirit worlds.

At present there are many souls in physical and non-physical states involved in finding ways to improve communication between the different states. It is important to bear in mind, though, that this has to be done, or, I should say, needs to be done with total respect for free will, so that souls in spirit do not interfere with the freedom of choice of those who are experiencing physical existence.

We have discussed ways and means of achieving easier communication with guides/guardian angels. Since you have been patient enough to continue to share our exploration, I'd like to invite you to accompany me in further experimentation and to assure you that it's a great privilege for me that you, dear reader, have agreed to participate, even to this stage, in our journey towards utopia. You may be interested to learn that in the relatively short time since we embarked on this communication, in 1981, much progress has been made through the efforts of many souls in raising awareness on a global scale.

Let's look at how you communicate with each other in the physical world. You talk, listen, sing, make music, laugh, smile, write, use technology (for example, telephones, radio, television, computers), advertise, make love, stay silent, make gestures, play games, fight, touch, give presents, paint, sculpt, cook, share material possessions, go into partnerships, reach out to each other in all sorts of ways. By and large, you accept all those forms of communication as a matter of course. Sometimes your communication is fully conscious, for example, making a telephone call, sometimes it isn't, for example, body language. In any case, it's all part of your daily living.

The main difference between physical and spirit states is that souls in spirit don't have to operate in form or structure; for example, they don't need language, as you know it; communication happens telepathically. That's just as well, you might say, as you can imagine the confusion there would be if souls in spirit, who are not confined by national boundaries or ethnic groupings, had to contend with language barriers. Anyway, all your languages and dialects resulted from limited, because physical, mobility; people in a particular region, who wouldn't have known of the existence of other areas, developed their own peculiar methods of communicating with each other. That doesn't mean that in spirit souls are deprived of sound. Those who like sound can have all they want of it; those who don't needn't tune into it. It's rather analogous to somebody using ear phones, listening to radio or television, having the benefit of sound without intruding on anybody else's silence.

Incidentally, if it weren't possible for souls in spirit to experience sound, you can easily imagine what a profound culture shock it would be for any of your present sound oriented younger generations who might find themselves catapulted (by "dying") into a soundless nonphysical state. Perish the thought!

Communication between guides and humans, as built into the grand design, needs to be unobtrusive. Essentially, a balance had to be found between giving help, and noninterference with free will. There's no rigidity in the grand design; it adjusts itself continuously to evolving consciousness. This adjustment is reflected in the form of communication considered desirable at any particular time.

The material in these sessions couldn't be given physical clothing without the cooperation of a human agent. At this stage on our journey, it seems to me that the time is right for us, together, to see how we can go further with breaking down the barriers of communication between the physical and spirit states. I would like to outline certain suggestions and considerations, some of which will be reminders of material already given but which I have included for ease of reference, and in order to provide a readily accessible "package."

1. It is hardly necessary to say that your acceptance of yourself as a spirit being, a soul who happens to have temporarily taken on physical form, is a basic first step.
2. Acceptance that you have guides who link in with you and whose purpose is to help you fulfill your potential is desirable.
3. Release yourself from conditioning as far as you can; in case this sounds like a tall order, see it in terms of being open-minded and non-judgmental without being controlled by rigid beliefs or absolutism.
4. The more relaxed you are the easier the flow of communication will be; anxiety, for example, trying too hard, creates a blockage.
5. Ask your guides to keep your aura free from negative energies; it would be an interference with your free will for your guides to do that without your consent; you need ask only once.
6. Consider how impressions come to you normally. For instance: Do you tend to get visual images easily? Do you operate more on a feeling level? Are you comfortable with ideas? Do you understand

things better when you write them down? Do you find that you just know things at times without having to go through a logical process to work them out? Your guides will tend to develop communication with you through your particular style.

7. The main difficulty with this sort of communication is how to know whether it's really happening. In your day-to-day life you meet people, you talk to them, they answer you, you can touch them, if you want to, and you have no doubt about that sort of reality. Similarly, you talk to somebody by telephone, or you hear somebody talking on radio, or see somebody on television, and you accept that that's real. Normally, you can't see or hear a guide in so obvious a way. How then can you know whether you're in direct communication with a guide or not?

8. You may remember that I used an analogy of a jigsaw puzzle to illustrate how all souls are linked together in consciousness (in God) but yet that each soul has its own unique place in the cosmic design. As you grow in awareness you tap into that consciousness more and more which is another way of saying that you integrate increasingly with you as oversoul. That is, of course, your overall purpose in coming into your present physical lifetime, and your guides are constantly helping you to fulfill that purpose. As your awareness increases, you are, to a continually magnifying extent, automatically in tune with your divine consciousness, so that your own feelings and thoughts are on a wavelength with those of your guides and of you yourself as oversoul. That's why you may not

feel guidance coming to you in an obvious manner as if from outside of you. You are allowing God to manifest in you, which is reflected in your feelings and thoughts.

9. Suppose you feel you have a decision to make about something. I'm taking it for granted that you have already gone through the steps which I have outlined above. You have asked your guides to help you with the decision, so you let go as far as you can of any preconceived ideas and wait and see what comes to you. This is where the considerations referred to at paragraph 6 above are relevant; an answer is likely to come to you in a way that suits your style. If no clear answer comes to you immediately, don't worry; sometimes the process of decision-making works out better when it's given breathing space. If your guides can't get through to you directly (for example, if you're too anxious), they will find other ways of reaching you, for example, through somebody else, or a dream, or by nudging you to read something or listen to a radio program.

10. The more you integrate with something, the less you notice it as separate. That's why people are often disappointed when they find that what began as very obvious communication with guides is no longer so; some people then start questioning themselves and wondering where they have "gone wrong." They haven't, of course; rather, they have "gone right"!

11. All the same you say, "I'd love to be able to have a chat with a guide occasionally in the same way as I would with a (human) friend. Why couldn't that be fitted into the grand design? Surely now that I've

taken all the preparatory steps you've outlined and I understand how guidance works, an occasional chat could only have the effect of helping me to increase my awareness?" You may not have any specific problem or pressure of decision-making at all, but you'd simply like to have a chat. Fair enough.

12. In the utopian state, communication between the spirit and physical worlds will be commonplace. Initially this will involve only a tiny proportion of the (physical) world's population. Even now, though, with the phenomenal acceleration in the movement of consciousness which has been taking place in recent years, many people are ready to cooperate in a venture (or, maybe more appropriately, an adventure) which will bring about dramatic change in people's perception of life and, indeed, in how they live.

13. I must remind you that what we're attempting now has never before happened on Earth. Many souls on this (noncorporeal) side have been waiting eagerly for enough souls on Earth to be ready to go ahead with experimentation in breaking down the barriers between the spirit and physical worlds. I'm not talking now about the occasional mediumistic communication which has flourished sporadically through the centuries, or about something "paranormal" which has hitherto been confined to a small number of people who have been regarded as particularly psychic or spiritual or more likely, "odd"; but rather about developments which will be open to all those who wish to prepare themselves to access them.

14. So, then, you're ready and willing to participate in this experimentation. What do you need to do?

How can you bring about a situation where you can have a chat with a guide or with a relative or friend who is now in spirit?

15. I would recommend that you initially confine yourself to experimenting with a guide. Later, as you see how you progress with that, you can, if you wish, ask your guide to facilitate the other type of communication for you. In general, it is desirable, in order to avoid interference with privacy, that communication with a "dead" friend or relative should only be arranged through a guide.

16. At present it is not possible for a guide to appear before you or beside you in a form that you can readily see and touch, so that you won't have the same immediate proof that you have with a physical associate. The situation is unbalanced as far as you are concerned in that the guide is more obviously aware of you than you are of the guide.

17. Given that physical presence is not feasible, communication has to be arranged rather like a telephone conversation minus the sound. (My analogy is with nonvisual telephonic communication.) When somebody contacts you by telephone you're aware of the caller before you can hear a voice, and you don't have to pinch yourself and ask, "Is it just my imagination playing tricks on me?" Before you lift the telephone you get a signal—the ringing tone—and you know that there's somebody at the other end of the line. Similarly, you can arrange to have a signaling system with a guide or guides which will be your way of satisfying yourself that you're having authentic communication.

18. Just to be clear—what we're talking about here is the situation at your end. Guides don't need any

signals in order to tune into you; as I've already said, they're only a thought away from you.

19. If you want to have a chat with a guide, I suggest that you ask for an agreed signal that you will continue to use as a lead-in to your communication. For example, Sara accepts that she has guides helping her on her human journey. She feels that she would like to establish a more conscious link with at least one of them. She relaxes as much as she can in whatever way best suits her and she sends a thought to her guides expressing her wish and asking for a signal. Because her visual faculties are strong, in other words, she understands something more easily when she can put a visual image on it, her guides will be likely to show her a picture, for example, of a flower, or a bird, or an animal, or an object that's familiar to her. Whenever, then, she "rings up" a guide and that image flashes on her "screen," she can accept that she's in a two-way communication with a guide.

20. For people who aren't comfortable, or don't feel confident, with visual images, other signals will be used, for example, a shivery or tingly feeling, a word, an impression of being touched, a feeling of an in-flow of energy or of being gently rocked. The main thing is that it should be an easy signal which would also be unmistakable.

21. While guides are, of course, friends, their aim is to help people regain lost awareness, so that will always be a primary consideration in their communication with you. You will notice that there's always subtlety in the guidance you receive, particularly as you progress in your intercourse.

Accordingly, don't expect matters to be set out for you in a black and white way. In the nature of things, you are more likely to wish to have communication with your guides when you want something; that's understandable because you're still struggling with humanity, while your guides have moved beyond that. All the same, you might bear in mind that your guides like to hear from you, too, when things are going smoothly for you; just to send greetings, or thanks, or love. They're not looking for gratitude, but it expands your energy when you express it.

Sexual Energy in "The New Consciousness"

"Can you redefine sexual energy and its present force in the new consciousness?"

Sex has been a potent force in the history of human evolution. I'm using the word "sex" here in terms of interaction between people rather than literally as gender. People enjoy it, become obsessed with it, abuse others through it, use it as a power base, run away from it, see it as a duty, sell it, sacrifice it to their God, consider themselves deprived if it doesn't figure in their lives, and, sometimes, if it does. One way or another it impinges on people's lives in significant ways.

I need to make a distinction here between sexual energy and what is known as sexual intercourse. It would be a basic mistake to think of sex exclusively in terms of a sexual act between two people. Its most obvious expression is as the source of procreation which has tended to create confusion in people's minds to the extent of either seeing its sole purpose in that light, or as a potentially pleasurable activity which incidentally has a procreative capacity. But many people, either through choice or through circumstances outside of their control, don't experience direct sexual interaction in the form of sexual intercourse. That doesn't mean, though, that their sexual energy is necessarily suppressed; it is, only if they allow themselves to become obsessed about the lack of such experience.

Fundamentally, sexual energy is about creativity. In the final analysis, what really affects people most, and limits them, is a lack of creative expression in their lives. Life on Earth is structured in such a way that people need money or its equivalent to survive. In order to obtain money people have to find remunerative employment or become dependent on social assistance of some kind unless they're amongst the favored few who have substantial private incomes. In many cases, most likely the vast majority, the work that people do in order to provide income for themselves and their families is, from their perspective, repetitive and unfulfilling; unfortunately, it's the exception rather than the rule for people to find their work both spiritually and financially rewarding.

In consideration of this question, the increasing impact of technology is significant. Amongst other things, technology is designed to take care of boring, routine tasks, and it does. It is, consequently, expected to leave people with time for more productive work. It certainly means that people have more time on their hands, but the challenge of finding income-producing work is often daunting, if not insuperable. Resulting worry, then, suppresses creativity.

An ideal would be utopian societies, nation/states, where all people would have available to them soul-satisfying outlets of expression without having to be concerned about survival in financial terms. That situation is not likely to be generally attainable for many years yet; but the more people can achieve it in individual ways, the sooner it will be.

To answer the question, I would redefine sexual energy as creativity. All people are creative; it's impossible for a part of God not to be creative. Sexual energy, then, is inseparably linked with the overall creativity of being, and that energy is present in everybody without exception. It can find outlets through all forms of creative expression, by which I mean, generally, how people approach whatever they do whether it be writing a book or a poem or a play, or painting a picture, or taking a photograph, or sculpting, or embroidery, or flower arranging, or gardening, or designing a building, or cooking, or computer programming, or healing in its many forms, or farming, or filmmaking, or acting, or sports, or traveling, or resting, or whatever form of activity presents itself for them. What I'm saying really is that all human activity has to be creative because all human beings are creative. Once they accept that, their self-esteem is raised, the flow of their energy is released, and opportunities for more and more self-expression become available to them.

Suppose you were in a situation where you'd never have to bother about earning money. What would you want to do with your life? Having answered the question, project the answer into your present income-needing situation.

For example, Paula is employed in a secretarial position which has long since ceased to offer her any challenge; that in itself, of course, is a tribute to her capacity in applying her organizational flair to the job. One day she decides to have a look at what she would really like to do. The answer she comes up with is that she'd love to be a journalist.

Apart from the fact that she can't afford to leave her job, she would have to go through a long process of training and there would be no guarantee that she would be acceptable as a candidate, let alone that she'd find an opportunity for employment. Is, then, this exercise of looking into what she'd want a waste of time? Paula has used her creative energy in her approach to her secretarial job. Now she needs to bring that energy into fulfilling her dream. Her job provides her with a cushion to help her on her way, perhaps to do a course in journalism, or creative writing, or to join a creative writing group. In her life experience, including her work, she may well find interesting material which she may be able to use as a basis for an article or a feature. Because she has her job so well organized, she may have some spare time during the day which she could devote to, say, research into a somewhat esoteric subject which might be of interest to many people. She has freedom to experiment because she's not dependent for survival on getting an income through journalism, so she can send her articles out to newspapers, magazines, etc.

If, as would be likely to happen, she only gets rejection slips or is ignored initially, she'll have the honor of sharing the early experience of most successful writers. Even if she never becomes a full-time journalist, she will have opened up for herself a vast outlet of creative expression and, in the process, brought a lot of enjoyment into her life, with the result that, incidentally, her secretarial job is now much more satisfying. Thus, her creative energy is no longer suppressed and she is more fully expressing herself, including her sexuality.

If I may move from the particular to the general then, what I'm suggesting is that people don't dismiss their dreams, their fantasies; that what may seem to be impossible, may be achievable in indirect ways and that their very situation which may seem to be totally restrictive, may in fact, help them on their way. Seeing things from a different perspective will free their energy, of which their sexuality is an integral part.

Akashic Records: What They Are

From time to time you have come across the expression "akashic records" as the title given to spirit (nonmaterial) records of the evolutionary journeys of souls on their individual paths. Are there, in fact, such records? If so, what form do they take? And how can they be explored?

In earlier times mention of records would have brought up images of mountains of paper, files, index cards, rows and rows of shelving, etc. More recently, computer technology has taken over and has made access to information immeasurably easier and faster, and has also overcome physical storage problems.

We're faced with a dilemma here in terms of communication. I have repeatedly said that in spiritual terms there's no past, so how can there be a record of something that doesn't exist? Spirituality always exists in the present. You, the soul, your feelings and thoughts, your consciousness, cannot be other than in the present. You have experiences from year to year, from month to month, from week to week, from day to day; you feel and think your way through them and they help to shape your consciousness. But you cannot exist in the past. From day to day, from hour to hour, even from moment to moment, inside yourself, in your feelings and thoughts, you can only live in the present; you simply cannot relive even the experience of a second ago. So it's true to say that in spiritual (real) terms there's no past. It's also true to say that for each soul there has been a history of past experiences, the effects of which exist in its present consciousness. I think you can see that there's no contradiction between the two statements.

Given that the grand design provides for the possibility of reincarnation, it would be strange if the design did not include facilities for each soul to study and evaluate the history of its progress towards the regaining of the awareness it lost. So, of course, there is such a record and it is the right of each soul to have access to it. The process of getting access is much more sophisticated and more simple than anything achievable in human technological terms. It happens through an unveiling of consciousness, like a film unfolding before one's eyes.

For example, Agnes leaves her body and, after a period of adjustment to her new state, decides that she would like to have a look at her previous history. She doesn't have to go anywhere or to be anywhere in particular in order to fulfill her wish. She might like to have a guide with her in order to help her assess her progress, but that's a matter for herself. All that's needed is that she should have reached such a level of awareness that her mind is not set in any pattern of rigid beliefs, for example, that she can accept the possibility of reincarnation, or that there's no such thing as a judgmental God. It would be easier for her if she were to ask a guide to help her. The guide would prompt her so that she would realize the extent of the information available to her; in other words, she could ask the guide to roll the film and give her a running commentary on it.

The information about Agnes's evolution (and every soul's) is stored in the universal consciousness, literally, in God. It's very difficult to explain that in human terms because consciousness doesn't have a tangible physical reality. It has permanence, though; so it can be said that it is eternally present, or that there's nothing but the present. Everything, every feeling, thought, action is stored eternally in divine consciousness; nothing is ever wiped out as sometimes happens with data stored in a computer. If that seems a bit frightening, don't worry; remember that there's no judgment. It's simply that all is God and God is all, infinitely and eternally, and no part of God can ever not *be*.

What about the poor human trying to get information about his evolutionary history? Much progress is being made towards making information available as helpfully as possible. A lot depends on how open people are to receiving such information. If people can accept that they have guides available to help them and if they practice communicating with their guides, they will be guided to the sources of information. Usually, what will be filtered to them is whatever is relevant to their present life. People who have developed their communication are helping others to do likewise. Once conditioning is released anything is possible.

The simple answers to the questions posed at the beginning of this session is that there are permanent records of all souls' evolutionary journeys, that the records are in divine consciousness, and, therefore, in each soul/oversoul; and that exploration is easier as souls grow in consciousness and can be significantly helped through communication with guides.

You can see, I hope, why self-forgiveness on the part of each soul is so fundamentally essential.

Part IV

Beings from Other Planets

Question: "Do beings from other planets inspire and direct us? Are they helping us move to the next dimension?"

I previously used an example of a soul choosing, for growth purposes, to experience temporary evolution on the planet Uranus. Earth is the only planet on which there is, at present, materialization, as you know it, although spirit life can simulate the conditions of Earth without its density of form.

It is very difficult for you to conceive of life existing outside of place or time. Even though you have never physically experienced life on other planets, you can accept that they exist because they have been absorbed into the structure of human comprehension. So it is easier for you to picture existence, whatever its form, centered in a place, albeit an unfamiliar one such as another planet, rather than existence in no place. It would follow then, I think, that guidance coming from (spirit) beings on other planets might have a more readily comprehensible ring to it than guidance coming from spirit beings who don't seem to have any base.

All creation, including all planets, exists for the use of souls who are always free to choose how they express themselves; in other words, at different stages they may choose to experience repeated lives on Earth or a combination of lives on Earth as well as on another or other planets. That means

159

that some souls who are now on Earth in physical bodies have also experienced life on other planets in nonphysical bodies. There are many "aliens" now living on Earth. There's nothing sinister about that, by the way; souls are souls, no matter what form their expression takes.

The grand design envisages that human beings are helped by guides specially assigned to them through their own choice. There are also guides, spirit beings, angels, archangels, whatever you like to call them, who are overseeing the operation of the planet generally, not in a controlling way, but always seeking to provide opportunities for growth in consciousness. As we have seen in other sessions, souls in spirit are constantly in communication with human beings; people's awareness of that depends on their openness and capacity to receive the communications. So of course, souls who happen to be on other planets communicate with, or try to communicate with, human beings. How inspirational the communications are depends on the levels of awareness of the communicators, as also does whether they attempt to direct, if that word is being used as meaning "control" rather than "guide."

At present, most souls now on Earth have not chosen to have guides specifically assigned to them. Accordingly, they are more open to indiscriminate communication from spirit sources, including those on other planets, than those who have so chosen. As you know, guidance is usually arranged before a soul takes on a physical body; but if at any time during a physical lifetime a person decides to ask for a guide or guides, there are billions of evolved souls who would love such assignments. When one soul is helped all souls are helped through the interlinking of consciousness.

The Atlantean Experiment

There has been a good deal of speculation regarding Atlantis, including as to whether it existed at all. There was such a place. In terms of your time it ceased to exist some 400,000 years ago.

While Atlantis was a land mass, it was different from the Earth as you know it. Atlanteans were not human as you are. They were, of course, spirit beings like you, but their bodies were not dense like yours.

Atlantis was an experiment which, if it had worked, would have shortened, considerably, the journey back to full awareness. It was designed as a model and a basis for a more extended form of evolution. There were about a hundred million souls altogether involved in the experiment, which lasted for a period of about 50,000 years.

It would, I think, be fair to describe the Atlantean experiment as a halfway state between life in spirit and life on Earth, as you know it. As I have said, Atlantis was a land mass, but it did not have vegetation such as the Earth now has. Neither did it initially have animal life, but experimentation with animal life, including birds, was subsequently introduced. The idea was that it would be inhabited by souls who had reached a fairly advanced stage of evolution and who would be subjected to some limitation of power by taking on bodies. In appearance the bodies were somewhat like your bodies, but there were no deformities, or color distinctions. They were male and female. They did not need food in order to survive, nor did they need transport in order to get from place to place; as in spirit, creation, including movement, was achieved through thought. Yet, both the land and the bodies had substance in the material sense of the word.

Atlantis was designed as a learning experience in a transitional way and there was no question of it being more than that. Ultimately, its undoing was that the old power hunger began to take over and some souls started a process of confusing appearance with reality; for example, they thought that immortality was attainable in Atlantis. They (rightly) concluded that life is energy, so they looked at sources of apparently ever-continuing energy, such as the sun. So why not tap that energy, focus it, and transfer it into their bodies? Much experimentation was carried out in that field, with crystals being the most common focal points. There was, and could be, only temporary success. Their mistake was that they did not understand that they were spiritual beings, a combination of feelings and thoughts merging into consciousness, who did not need any external trappings, such as physical bodies, to achieve immortality. They were, of course, already immortal, but either were not aware of that or wanted immortality within the conditions which they had created for themselves in Atlantis. (The search for physical immortality has continued through subsequent civilizations, and, indeed, the doctrine of the resurrection of the body on "the last day," which is enshrined in some religious belief systems, stems from that search.)

All souls, as spirit beings, have unlimited power. In their ultimate state of total awareness they use that power with complete respect for each and every other soul. All the pain and trauma of the fall from awareness and the journey back to awareness have resulted from the abuse of power. Atlantis was designed as a vehicle for increasing awareness through limitation of power, which would have the effect that souls would have to learn to interact with, and relate to, each other with respect and cooperation. As things turned out, the Atlantean situation was not restrictive enough. The souls taking part in the experiment remembered too much of their spirit state and the demonstration of what might loosely be termed magic/psychic tricks; in other words, external manifestation of power became an end in itself.

What happened to Atlantis? It was a democracy with its own government, which consisted of a council of representatives selected by the people. In theory, the council was subject to periodic change. In practice, that did not happen in that, within a relatively short period of time, there was a distinct ruling class which began to revel more and more in the trappings of power.

Tyranny breeds rebellion. The free spirit does not want to be caged. So, as the rulers became more autocratic, counter movements started. Conflict, repression, isolation, cruelty, violent deaths, all the things that are so familiar to your world, followed. Inevitably, what started out as an idealistic revolution turned into a power struggle, with both sides becoming equally obsessed with the use (abuse) of power although, of course, they would have recoiled from the idea that they were bedfellows. In any event, it became clear with the passage of time that Atlantis was a doomed civilization. The grand designers felt that developments were too closely following the pattern of the earlier fall from awareness and decided that a fresh start with a more limited human expression was desirable. Accordingly, Atlantis was allowed to "self-destruct," which was the inevitable result of its own advanced knowledge combined with power obsession. For the modern equivalent, you have only to consider two superpowers competing for world domination with technology capable of achieving unlimited destruction available to both of them. When each side wanted to dominate the other and each side was convinced of its own invincibility, then there could only be one outcome, given the capacity for destruction available to both sides. So Atlantis literally destroyed itself.

Most of the former inhabitants of Atlantis are, at present, on Earth and are to the forefront in advanced consciousness growth areas. In the evolutionary process, which they have undergone since Atlantis, they have, to a large extent, learned the lessons posed by the Atlantean experience.

Earth, as you know it, was deliberately designed as a more restrictive experience so that access to power would be less easily attainable. Nonetheless, the pursuit of power has been obsessive for many people, and not only the people who have achieved notoriety. The obsession has operated, and continues to operate, in the interaction of personal relationships and, perhaps most insidiously, in the intimacy of one-to-one relationships.

The purpose of the Atlantean experiment, as is the purpose of planet Earth as it now exists, was to help souls to shed the mud of unawareness. As I have already said, Atlantis was intended as a model which could be expanded upon. It failed as a model, but not as an experiment, in that the design of a more restrictive form of Earth life which would, it was hoped, enable progress to be made more surely, if more slowly, followed from it. The stage has now been reached on planet Earth, of course, that, technologically, it has the capacity to destroy itself, or, rather, be destroyed by opposing forces. However, I don't foresee that happening.

My main purpose in this session is to focus on growth of awareness, or enlightenment, which is a commonly used word in this context. Souls would have been saved much pain if the Atlantean model had worked as a model. It didn't work because, essentially, enlightenment came to be equated with power. A miracle worker is an obvious example of somebody who has power. Does it automatically follow that the miracle worker is enlightened? If not, from where does he derive his power?

Many evolved souls have, through the centuries, come to Earth and performed miracles; in other words, they have achieved results which are not normally possible within the limits of human endeavor. What feats have come to be classified as miracles were commonplace in Atlantis. All the Earth miracle workers were and are former Atlanteans. They were, and are, not necessarily more enlightened than many other souls whose life purposes were, and are, fulfilled in obscurity. They have recognized (as other nonmiracle workers also have) that physical manifestation is ultimately an illusion and that spiritual life is the only reality. This recognition enabled/enables them to transcend the normal limitations of Earth. They simply did not accept/do not accept those limitations.

At the same time, no human being has ever been able to perform what you would classify a miracle without the aid of spirit helpers. At different times it has served the purpose of the grand design that miracles should be performed and the agent to fulfill that purpose has agreed to be born into Earth. It is, and always has been, a delicate mission. The agent is placed in a powerful position and needs to have evolved into a deep and permanent sense of his own reality as a part of God equal to, but no better than, every other part, if he is to escape the recurring trap of power (egotism).

As his awareness grows, or, more accurately, as his unawareness diminishes, the spiritual traveler will be more and more conscious that he has access to all the evolved energy of the universe, but that that consciousness does not give him any right to set himself above others or to exert dominion over them. Accordingly, he will not seek to set himself up as a guru, or a cult figure. In saying that, I don't mean to make any judgment on personalities who, during the course of the Earth's evolution, have become cult figures, some of whom have had profound influence on the pattern of that evolution. There's a world of difference between seeking preeminence and having it attributed to you. Souls cannot avoid sharing what they are. They do so either negatively or positively, in a limited way or widely. The more they accept themselves for what they are, the extent of their sharing of themselves inevitably widens. They are "ordinary" souls in the sense that they are equal (in God) with all other souls. But they are extraordinary human beings which may often be a source of confusion until one accepts the transitional and illusory nature of humanity.

What Is Life on Planet Earth Going to Be Like in the Future?

I

You would like me to outline in some detail how I see the future of planet Earth. I hasten to say that what I'm giving here is my vision of how the planet will ideally evolve, and I'm stressing that it's my vision and not an immutable pattern of evolution. As you know, the existence of free will makes it impossible to say in a black and white way that this is how it's all going to be. Nonetheless, my vision is in line with the aims of the grand design and the trend of its implementation.

It is quite clear, I think, that the pace of evolution has accelerated to a remarkable degree in the twentieth century. This has reflected itself very obviously in the technological revolution that has taken place. What has been happening in the field of technology is part of an overall changing consciousness which has been exciting for many people, disturbing for many others, and both exciting and disturbing for still many others. Institutional arrangements, which had seemed to be unbreachable in their solidity, have been rocked to their foundations; leadership has had to find new expression. People are no longer prepared to accept that their lives can be controlled within rigid frameworks of rules and regulations; the emphasis on finding individual freedom of expression has radically increased. Inevitably, of course, there's a backlash. What has come to be called fundamentalism is stretching out its tentacles to clutch within its grasping arms those who are still looking for security in being told this you must do or this you must not do, so that you will forever be rewarded or punished depending on how you behave yourself.

Understandably, given all the changes that have been taking place, it was a century of many contrasts. There were wars on a scale that the world has never before experienced. People behaved, and are still behaving, towards each other with cruelty of such proportions that it is almost inconceivable how free will could, and can, be exercised in such horrific ways. On the other hand, many barriers of rigid class distinctions (which were the source of widespread, but seemingly socially respectable and acceptable, forms of cruelty for many centuries) have been broken down. Governmental systems have apparently become increasingly democratic, admittedly not without much struggle and bloodshed, in many cases. Most significantly, the level and the extent of worldwide communication processes have increased so dramatically that news of what's happening almost anywhere in the world is now, more or less, instantly available. Injustices, barbarities, atrocities, man's inhumanity to man, are now highlighted to such an extent that nobody, no matter how secure his position seems to be, can any longer be sure of escaping detection if he is a participant in such activities.

What tends to be considered newsworthy, of course, is still, generally, negatively focused. What are regarded as scandalous happenings create more sensational headlines than recording the achievements of so many who are

unobtrusively working to help people find peace and fulfillment in their lives. Accordingly, it would be superficially
reasonable for someone who regularly reads newspapers,
and/or looks and listens to television, and/or listens to the
radio, to conclude that the state of the world is getting worse
rather than better. Yet, in my view, there is no doubt but that
planet Earth is now an infinitely better place in which to live
than it has ever been. Platforms are now being provided for
people who are at present experiencing life on Earth, and
for those being born and to be born into physical bodies, to
create states of being which could literally be described as
heaven on Earth. What sort of states will those be?

Once again, I think it would be helpful to attempt to
answer that question by way of an illustration.

II

Because of the breakthrough in consciousness that has
been taking place in recent times and is continuing to happen, the key to which is acceptance of divinity in humanity,
in other words, no separation from God/love, it is now possible to envisage a state within the physical system that
would serve as a model for the further evolution of Earth in
the fulfillment of its purpose of helping souls to regain lost
awareness. This would not be a recreation of the Atlantean
model, although it would have fundamentally the same motivation.

In the context of the illustration it is appropriate not to
pinpoint an existing identifiable location. The word "utopia"
has been incorporated into everyday language and is taken
to mean an ideal condition or situation. So it would suit, I
think, to call our model state utopia.

I'm going to use the present tense in describing utopia
even though I'm giving it a birth date thirty years into the
future. I'm doing this in the interests of simplicity and easy

reading as well as to give the new state an immediacy of existence.

Utopia is a small country with a population of about four million people. It is not a new country, but it was divided under different governmental jurisdictions until 2025 when it was reunited into one state. It is entirely independent in its administration of its own affairs.

It so happened, and, of course, this was no accident, that the people who inhabit the new state were at the forefront of the emerging consciousness of the twentieth century. Souls tend to reincarnate in groups, sometimes quite large groups. It was part of the purpose of the souls who were born into that location, or who moved into it from other areas, during the later twentieth and early twenty-first centuries, that they should create a way of being in the physical dimension which would mirror, as far as possible, life in spirit at the fourth stage of evolutionary growth and which, ideally, might be an inspiration to others. Thus all the inequalities, injustices, deprivation and pain, which still, unfortunately, are inherent in the human experience, would more quickly be eradicated so that the planet would no longer be a vale of tears, but a joyful interlude in unfolding consciousness.

Initially, when the new utopian state came into being, it inherited a governmental system that followed broadly the outline of twentieth century democracies. For example, it had a president and a parliament, all elected for specific terms by the votes of the people. The membership of the parliament consisted of representatives of different political groupings who presented themselves and their policies to the people; the numerical parliamentary strength of each party was dependent on its popularity with the electorate. The aim of each party was to have an overall majority so that it could form a government on its own. If, after an election, no party emerged with such a majority, the alternatives were to form a coalition of two or more parties, or to hold another election.

The president was also elected by popular vote and was the first citizen, with prescribed constitutional powers.

There were institutions of state which were outside of the political system but subject to political heads who formed the membership of the government. These included the civil service and security arrangements, for example, policing, military, and custodial. Courts of law were independent bodies in the execution of their jurisdiction, although not insofar as the appointment of the judiciary was concerned; in practice, the government exercised that function.

In theory, all power was vested in the people. In practice, this was so insofar as the people, by their votes, decided who should exercise that power on their behalf.

In earlier times the spread of population was rurally oriented, but as the twentieth century progressed people moved to cities in large numbers. Major adjustments were required in the provision of amenities, such as, housing, transport, medical facilities, water, sewerage, electricity, heating, telecommunications, employment, welfare. The shift towards urbanization marked a radical departure from a society, where generally everybody within a community knew everybody else, to a more anonymous way of life, which suited some people and didn't suit others.

Religions were mainly Christian in denomination with small minority groupings, such as, Jewish, Buddhist. The Christian religions were mainly Roman Catholic, Anglican, Presbyterian, Methodist. Traditionally, there were many tensions between the Roman Catholic and the other Christian religions. The hierarchical authoritarianism of the Roman Catholic religion and the biblical fundamentalism of some of the other religions were severely tested and dented as the twentieth century drew to a close.

While the democratic system did not, in theory, allow for class distinctions, there were many inequalities; for example, large numbers of people could not find remunerative employment and had to survive on meager welfare allowances. Pyramidal hierarchical structures were the order of the day, with, inevitably, the vast majority of workers serving at the bases of the pyramids and finding little fulfillment in their work. Many people, particularly older people, lived in isolated penury. The poverty of external circumstances often tended to create spiritual aridity which was not helped by easy answers to the effect that suffering was the way to find happiness in a heaven which was impossible to conceptualize.

III

For the sake of clarity and simplicity I divided the process of the different stages in a soul's journeying to a state of full awareness into seven stages, with the seventh being the ultimate one. The first and second stages combine a mixture of continuity of life in physical and nonphysical bodies. Souls who reach the fourth stage still, if they wish, incarnate/reincarnate in physical bodies; they do so with the object of helping others to grow in consciousness.

What's happening in the present shift in consciousness is that the spiritual and physical worlds are being moved closer together. It's much easier now than it would have been even as recently as twenty years ago to envisage a time when the barriers between the worlds will be broken down completely, as they are partially at present, and continuing communication will be possible (although maybe not always desired) between souls still in physical bodies and those who have left the physical scene (at least temporarily).

In describing the fourth stage earlier, I concentrated mainly on the guidance aspect of it; how souls at that stage act as guides to human beings. What I'd like to do now is to take the process further by describing in some detail how life functions at the fourth stage in its spirit manifestation and then to endeavor to represent how all that transfers to our utopian state. Utopia couldn't work in physical terms if the people inhabiting it hadn't reached the level of awareness of the fourth stage.

IV

First things first. Souls at the fourth stage fully accept their own divinity; they are in God, God is in them, there's no separation. They don't have any physical problems, such as, illness, tiredness, aging, disability, the need for food, clothing, shelter, money. Obviously all that makes a big difference. In a real sense, there's no government, no religion, no bureaucratic institutions, no laws, no rules or regulations, and no traffic jams!

In talking about souls at the fourth stage I'm really referring to oversouls; souls expressing their fullness of being, of consciousness. They have ready access to all knowledge, so that, of course, there's no need—I stress the word need—for schools or colleges or universities as vehicles of learning. Memory, as you know it within the physical system, is no longer necessary. Souls are identifiable in their individuality and appearance. Of course, they don't have material bodies but they appear to each other in forms which are expressive of the essence of each soul in its uniqueness.

In order to attempt to make life at the fourth stage comprehensible to you I'll have to use an approach of comparison with what you know.

The range of people's activities on Earth is multi-aspected. The following are some examples, in no presumed order of preference, of how people find satisfaction and enjoyment and fulfillment: reading, writing, painting, photography, film-making, film-viewing, gardening, walking, swimming, athletics, cooking, travel, holidays, sleeping, eating, drinking, television, radio, nature, driving, flying, making money, winning prizes, toys, farming, successful business deals, achieving recognition in their careers, loving relationship with children/adults/animals, solitude, being at peace with themselves and the world around them, causes, charities, material comforts, shopping, homemaking, giving and receiving gifts, special occasions, football matches, concerts, birthdays, weddings, ideas, discussion, listening to music, politics, horse/motor/cycle racing, playing golf, cards, crosswords, computers, technology generally, wood carving, sculpture, pottery, tapestry, relaxing, massage, therapeutic activities generally, design, invention, scholarship, skilled workmanship, acting, appearance, making clothes, jewelry, religious practices, meditation, making love, intimacy, communicating with their guides/guardian angels, feeling at one with God/love.

There are many others that I deliberately didn't include, such as, gambling, drug-taking, alcoholism, quarreling, physical fighting, accumulating possessions, robbery, gossiping, pornography, abuse, domination, manipulation, cheating, hunting, one-up-manship, bigotry, dogmatism, sexual promiscuity, exclusivity, prostitution, violence generally. While aspects of some of these may be present in my earlier list of examples, it is doubtful, I suggest, that they could be seen as meeting all three categories of satisfaction, enjoyment and fulfillment; temporarily, maybe, but not indefinitely.

It would be strange indeed if life in spirit were to be so totally different from life on Earth that forms of expression which occasion enjoyment on Earth would no longer be possible in spirit. (When I use the expression "in spirit" in this chapter I mean the fourth stage.) A logical expectation, I assume, would be that people would find much more expanded possibilities of fulfillment within the areas that interest them. The question is how?

In order to answer the question as clearly as I can, I propose to concentrate on certain areas which are of broad general relevance to human beings. I'm using "you" in a general way.

Artistic expression:

Suppose you are interested in reading novels where a large contributory factor to your enjoyment is in the unfolding of the stories. If you knew how the story was going to end before you started reading a book, a lot of the pleasure of the experience would be taken from you. In fact, you would probably be annoyed if somebody told you the outcome of the story before you had a chance to read it. The same thing is true of looking at a movie, or listening to, say, a radio play, or being a spectator at a sporting event, or, indeed, anything where the evolving experience is filled with expectancy. If, in spirit, there's no beginning and no ending, and you know it all anyway, how can you get the same, not to mention more, enjoyment from reading, looking at movies, etc.?

The simple answer is that in spirit everything is the way you want it to be. As you know, even within the space of one lifetime on Earth, your tastes in what brings you enjoyment, for example, literature, are continually evolving. That's also true in spirit. If you want to read a novel and you don't want to know how it ends, you can have that experience. You have unlimited ability to create whatever you wish, including temporary suspension of your awareness/insight/knowledge. It is unimaginable that somebody who enjoys, say, words, languages, the look and the feeling of books, would be deprived of that pleasure. There's no problem with words or with languages in spirit. Even though they are not necessary for communication, since that's achieved in more complete ways without them, yet they are available, of course, since everything is in whatever form you wish. You can have a most wonderful library, with beautifully bound books, if you so desire. If you have written books while on Earth, you can have them on your shelves, if you like. The books and the bookshelves are not material, but they are real; and real in a permanent way, if that's what you want, not in a temporary state as on Earth.

I imagine you can easily understand that what applies to books equally applies to, say, movies or television or radio or painting or writing or sculpting or pottery or wood carving or carpentry or music or choreography or flower arranging or design or gardening or cooking or sports or any and every artistic expression, including vehicles for such expression, for example, theaters, cinemas, wood. You can approach any of them at whatever level you like.

Sexual expression:

I've put this into a separate category because it occupies such a significant place in human existence.

As you know, the division of the human race into male and female genders was incorporated into the grand design not alone for procreative purposes but also as an aid to growth in consciousness, The possibility of reincarnation allows for a variety of experience through male and female lives on Earth.

When souls reach the fourth stage, the sexual distinction between male and female is no longer needed. But what if you wish to retain it? Then, of course, that's possible. Sexual expression is, ideally, about achieving unity, a depth of intimate communication. I talked in an earlier session about special relationships. The most exquisite, ecstatic union is achievable in spirit. In your human state you can have loving relationships with many people but you continually search for a soul mate as the ultimate in sexual intimacy. In spirit there is complete unity of communication in the most intimate possible ways with your soul mate. There's no such institution as marriage in spirit. There's no need for the rules of conduct that human societies seem to find necessary to establish.

Religious expression:

For many people, religious expression is a way of life. The human evolution has given birth to a great variety of religions. I need hardly dwell on how much energy has gone into religious devotion, with all its rituals, dogmas, rules, institutions, hierarchies, provision of places of worship, security, altruism, bigotry, intolerance, cruelty, division, solicitude; so much conflicting manifestation. The central difficulty about religions, and it is a fundamental, inescapable difficulty, is that they haven't come to terms with God. They teach that God is omnipotent, omniscient, omnipresent, that "man is created in the image of God" but the meaning of all that seems to elude them. In any case, God does not exist in terms of a Supreme Being, but is, rather, the divinity in all souls and in all creativity and all creation endlessly evolving, incapable of limitation. Souls in spirit are fully aware of this, and that awareness is part of their being, so that they are at one with God. That's the ever constant search for humans of course; the search for the lost God in them or, more accurately, the imprisoned God.

Well, you are now familiar with the pattern. Souls in spirit can have all the religious expression they want with whatever attendant rituals they would like to have. They know (at the fourth stage, I repeat, in case of confusion) that it's all a game.

Political expression:

Physical restrictions have developed a perception of the desirability of ordered societies on Earth. For example, people's needs for money, shelter, food, transport, roads, schools, hospitals, shops, had to be met. Increased urbanization has involved the introduction of systems for the ordered flow of traffic through, for example, traffic lights. There are always people who, for varying reasons, want to be regulators. Thus what has come to be known as politics evolved with all its institutional frameworks.

The same needs do not exist in spirit. So monarchs, presidents, governments, civil service, courts, security arrangements, all the incidental trappings with which you are familiar, are not alone unnecessary but, insofar as they are sources of elitism, would imply class distinction or orders of precedence which have no place in spirit.

As you know, some people love politics, whether as active participants or backstage debaters. How could they possibly enjoy themselves in spirit if there was no scope for political expression?

Here again, all things are possible. An analogy would be helpful, I think. You know how children love to invent games. They play the games with great intensity and seriousness and enjoyment but they also know, although they have suspended that knowledge, that they are playing games. Adults in the physical world have lost so much of what they had as children. People are born as children to give them fresh opportunities, yes, but also because they carry with them familiarity with the world of spirit while being temporarily free from the clutter of conditioning.

So, while there are no children in spirit (bear in mind that I'm using the expression "in spirit" to describe the fourth stage), souls can, if they wish, become as children and play whatever games they like with deep levels of passion, but they know they are playing games; they, too, have just suspended that knowledge while they are involved in the games.

Sporting expression:

I mentioned sports in the artistic section but I'm giving them a special category of their own because they occupy such a central place in the lives of so many people that they would be loath even to try to imagine any state of being that would not allow them to continue that interest. For those who wish to participate in sporting activities, the hard work, such as training, can be eliminated and they can just get on with playing the games. There's no difficulty about getting teams together, who can create their own rules and limitations for the duration of the games. Again, of course, they all know that they're only playing games, but that doesn't interfere with the spirit of the play (excuse the pun). You can participate in leagues and/or cups and/or tournaments to your soul's desire. You can also, of course, enjoy being a spectator, if you so wish.

Spiritual expression:

I only include this as a category in the interest of clarity. All expression is, of course, spiritual. As I have already said, souls in spirit fully accept themselves and their own divinity, so there's never any separation from God, no matter what games they play. Accordingly, there can be no intolerance, no judgmentalism, no attempts to control or dominate; just unconditional love in practice.

V

I should mention here that while the physical system is a vehicle for growth in awareness, it is also intended to be, in its evolution, a paradise or a divine playground. That will only be achieved if and when the fourth stage can be brought fully into human manifestation. I have chosen to use an example of an imaginary utopian state for illustration purposes, but that's not intended to promote elitism, or the idea of a specially chosen race; obviously, what we're really talking about is a state of consciousness, of being, which is independent of location and not limited in any way. At the same time, there's a gradualism in the way things evolve in the physical world; so it is well to pinpoint some location and start from there.

Now for the big question; how can the spirit and human states merge in our utopia?

VI

The primary ingredient is awareness, or consciousness. As I have already said, the people who inhabit utopia in the year 2025 are fully aware of themselves and accept themselves and their own divinity within their humanness. They have come together in accordance with arrangements made before they reincarnated. Their aim is to bring the fourth stage into human existence.

Since they are now in physical bodies they are subject to the restrictiveness that that involves. Accordingly, there will still have to be arrangements by which people can cooperate with each other in creating opportunities for all to live satisfying, fulfilling, and enjoyable lives. A comprehensive process of reform is set in motion once the new state is born.

A fundamental premise of the new setup is that there are, and will be, no hierarchies, no discrimination, no deprivation. It is a truism that power corrupts, and hierarchical systems inevitably lead to abuse of power. This was basically the reason for the original fall from awareness, the separation from God, which must never be allowed to happen again (with due respect to free will, of course).

Work features, naturally, but it is seen as creative expression, not as labor. All the people in the state, without exception, are provided with opportunities to experience fulfilling employment or no employment, if that's their wish. However, it's the nature of soul to have areas of interest, so that it will always find outlets for its creativity once it has the freedom to do so.

But, you ask, how can some form of hierarchical establishment be avoided since, in order to initiate reforms, or, indeed, to make anything happen at all, there have to be leaders or, at least, one leader?

To enable the new state to come into being, some people had to take initiatives. Those people were some of the participants in the governments of the previously fragmented state. Because they reached an awareness of their purpose, they set about abolishing and/or changing, in a gradual process, the existing systems, including their own positions. They explained through the communications media that utopia came into being in a spirit of true democracy, which meant that each person would be, ideally, his own government, and that now was the time to bring the ideal into reality, subject, of course, to the agreement of all the people, not just a majority.

The basic principle of each person being his own government implied that there would be no centralization of government, no laws, no controls; and that all organizations, systems, etc., within the state would be operable under shared arrangements, i.e., that all those involved in an organization would be, as it were, equal shareholders in it. There were, of course, many existing enterprises in the state which were privately owned. There was no question of any one person or group of people imposing a radical new system on anybody, as, indeed, there was no such thing as a new system, as such, with all its implications of people being asked to behave or conform in specified ways; rather the reverse, since it was the central philosophy of the new state that there would be no interference with individual freedom. What was being promulgated was a new way for people to live and interact together both as individuals, with total respect for each other's privacy, and as participants in group activities, whatever they might be, without having to cloister themselves off in isolated communities, or ashrams, or such-like.

There was a transitional period of about five years while people discussed, through television, radio, newspapers, seminars, etc., how a modem state might operate effectively in a totally democratic way without all the usual institutional trappings and incidental bureaucracies. Being able to manage it in spirit was one thing; achieving it within the restrictiveness of a physical system was something else again. It was no help that commentators from other countries saw what was happening in utopia as either madness or a recipe for total chaos; their more or less unanimous views were that human nature would make the whole idea unworkable.

Nonetheless, as we approach the year 2030, the new utopia is well established, with a hundred percent support, through a referendum, of its citizens. So, now, let's have a look at how it works.

VII

Some people are interested in nature, including farming. Their approach is on the lines of what you call organic farming. They bring their love of nature to bear on the whole operation and all nature responds to them. They produce wonderfully healthy food with an economy of space and effort. Do they own land? Yes, they do. How do they acquire land, if they haven't already got some? By negotiating with somebody who already has land and arriving at a mutually satisfactory way of exchange (subject, of course, to the owner being willing to sell). Houses, and property generally, change hands in an equally simple manner. There's no need to register ownership, nor are there any legal or taxation costs. Nobody even thinks of cheating or taking what belongs to another.

The inhabitants of utopia continue to use money because it's convenient, in their view, for them to do so. They have highly developed technological aids in order to make daily living easier and to allow people time to expand their own particular fields of interest.

Money is generated in many different ways; for example, through exports to other countries of farm produce (very much in demand because of its remarkable quality); artistic output (for example, many writers, painters, sculptors, craft workers, moviemakers, photographers, designers, actors, sports stars, musicians, singers, etc.); tourism (the rest of the world becomes increasingly curious about what's happening in utopia in spite of the initial skepticism of commentators); technological and consultancy expertise (past masters at finding ways to short-circuit procedures); industrial aids (some are interested in manufacturing equipment for use in different industries). Internally, there's much exchange of money for products and services.

But, you say, there must be some regulatory systems. How are markets generated abroad? The utopians must have banks, surely? How do people who are unable to work get money? There have to be employers and employees? What about taxation—there has to be, hasn't there?

It's interesting how central a part money plays in people's thoughts when one starts to look at how to create a different way of life on Earth; all the questions keep returning to it in some form.

No doubt you will have noticed how dynamic and powerful groups–small, medium, or large–can be when the people in them are on the same wavelength. We know that all the people in utopia are on the same wavelength, even though they have, of course, their own unique and individual ways of expressing their creativity. As I mentioned earlier, they have come on Earth in order to serve and to guide humanity, to create a model to show how life on Earth can be lived happily. They have not come as miracle workers or to be seen as exempt from the ordinary experiences and limitations of humanity, for example, illness, aging. So they are presented with the challenges of being human in the same way as all other humans although, admittedly, with the advantages of greater awareness and a more clearly perceived purpose.

It was obvious to them that money should be seen simply as energy with its place in the overall flow of energy, and that, therefore, it should be taken out of its existing predominant role. Consequently, all banks became redundant in the sense of their traditional functioning except for what might be called a central bank; also there would be no more taxation.

I have already referred in a general way to agriculture. The farmers, of course, produce food for home consumption as well as for export. They don't have employees. They have advanced technological equipment, and, when necessary, they come together in groups to accomplish certain tasks. A group will help one farmer one day, that farmer will join the group to help another member of the group on a different occasion, and so on. People who may like to experience farm life temporarily are usually facilitated by farmers, who, in turn, get willing helpers–if not always competent ones!

The farmers sell their produce to what I'll call cooperative stores (which, in turn, supply shops and arrange exports). The food that they produce satisfies some of their own needs. They use the money that they get from the stores to buy whatever else they require, such as clothes, equipment, entertainment, etc.

Animals, and, of course, birds, feature prominently in the state and are much loved. There are no practices such as fox hunting, or hare coursing, or badger baiting. There's no zoo. Vegetarianism is not a rule (there are no rules) but is widely practiced. If animals are killed for the purpose of providing food, it is done with love and respect. There are no slaughterhouses; whatever killing is done is carried out in the animal's own natural habitat. Animals are not exported for slaughter, nor is there any buying or selling of them.

The cooperative stores act as types of clearing houses. They supply shops and arrange exports. They are owned and managed by groups of people who are interested in that type of work and each of whom has his own special part to play in the enterprises. They have no hierarchical management structures; those involved act as committees with each member accepting responsibility for a particular area. Some members travel to other countries in connection with marketing of exports, although in general, that's not necessary because the products are so much in demand due to their excellence. The reception and entertainment of trade missions from abroad are the responsibility of designated committee members who choose that function.

How do the stores get money to pay the farmers and the salaries of their management groups? From the shops and from the export trade.

There's a wide variety of shops, some very small, some large, and some in between. The utopians are generally not much interested in possessions for the sake of possessions. Their houses are tastefully furnished without elaboration; they believe very much in keeping everything as simple as possible.

They live comfortably but not ostentatiously. Some of them, particularly the women, like jewelry, although most of them seem to wear it sparingly, but to great effect, I would say. They tend to wear clothes that suit their own style and temperament, rather than in response to any fashion trends. Observers or tourists from other countries are often fascinated by the complete lack of uniformity in dress of the utopians; many of the men, as well as the women, are dressed in resplendent colors. There's a great sense of joy and liberation about the way the people wear clothing: incidentally, that also extends to how they dress for business or what might be seen as formal occasions. Their houses, too, reflect their individual styles; even if from the outside there may sometimes be an apparent appearance of uniformity in the construction of the houses, internally, they are all arranged in accordance with the wishes of their occupants without any pressure in terms of how they might appear to neighbors or visitors.

The shops are owned and managed by individual families or by larger groups. Insofar as the bigger shops are concerned the same system applies as in the case of the cooperative stores, i.e., committees, with each member having his own particular area of responsibility. It's not a question of the utopians having decided to adopt an "across the board" uniform system of running their businesses, but they have found in practice that cooperating with each other on committee or group bases suits them. The committees arrange regular coordinating meetings to overview progress. Money? They get it from their customers.

Is there competition between the shops? Do some of them engage in price cutting in order to attract customers?

Since there are no regulatory laws or rules there are no trading restrictions on shops. It's an entirely open market economy. However, in practice there's no need for competition. People buy what they want where they want to, and they have enough money to do so. The people who manage the shops are not interested in competing with each other; it's not in their nature to be like that. Their real aim is to be happy in their lives, which includes the work they're doing, and to help all others similarly insofar as they can.

There are many hotels in utopia which are becoming increasingly busy because of the expansion in tourism. The hotels are also owned and managed by committees. There is a central tourism committee to coordinate matters affecting the industry generally; the committee also arranges for the issue of passports to those who require them.

VIII

At this stage you may be inclined to ask, "What's so different about all this?" For example, in a hotel some people will still have to do the routine jobs, such as, reception, cooking, cleaning, waiting tables, and they can't all be on management committees; even if they were, surely someone would have to allocate functions?

If you think about it, what's happening in utopia isn't, indeed, all that radically different from the trends of the twentieth-century evolution. People are finding, increasingly, that coming together into groups periodically is significantly helping them spiritually; in other words, they are finding it an effective way to come to terms with, and to feel good about, themselves. The problem is that they still have to survive, and for that they need money, which means that somehow money has to be generated. And, in the vast majority of cases, the work that people have to do in order to get money does nothing for them spiritually.

Yes, there are still the routine day-to-day tasks to be carried out in the utopian hotels (and all their other enterprises) and, even though they take every advantage of their technological aids, there are many jobs that only people can do and that it is important that people should do; for example, the energy that people put into cooking or making beds or waiting tables is a most influential ingredient in how the people at the receiving end feel.

You may recall that I intimated that activities do not have relative importance in themselves. They accrue value because of the effects they have on the performers. The utopians are at a level of awareness where they understand that principle. They are there to serve humanity, but they are not there as menials working long hours for meager wages. They are there in their own right as co-owners of the enterprises with which they happen to be involved (co-creators of the universe). So all the people who run the hotels, large or small, have equal shares in the ownership of the hotels. Tasks are allocated by choice and are, of course, subject to rotation, if people so wish. There's never any difficulty about demarcation of work. The accountant today could be peeling potatoes next year; but people's aptitudes and wishes are taken into account so that nobody is ever compelled to perform work that they find repellent to them. In fact, that couldn't arise anyway. Who would do the compelling?

What's happening in utopia is that people brought into the workplaces spirit, unity of purpose and enjoyment that you see operating in voluntary groupings at present and, most important, the opportunities and the environment have been created to allow them to do that.

I need hardly go into detail about the other utopian enterprises, such as manufacturing industries. By choice, they are all operated on the same principle of co-ownership, with all the workers forming committees of management. If you're thinking that this arrangement could entail very unwieldy committees, it doesn't; they split up into subcommittees, as considered desirable.

Doesn't the central principle of each utopian being his own government conflict with the seemingly uniform committee system which appears like a form of decentralized government? No, there's no conflict. As I have said earlier, each person has complete freedom about what type of work he will do or, indeed, whether to do any work at all. This is not usual except through illness or old age or incapacity of some kind. There's no unemployment, even if that means that some people work shorter hours. Nobody is ever sacked or compulsorily retired; people make their own choices as to whether or how long they stay in particular jobs. Nobody imposes standard work practices on anybody; each person works to his own style and has unlimited scope as to how he fulfills his role. Individuals come together in common endeavor without sacrificing their individuality in any way.

IX

Here I will deal with the big question of money and how it is managed.

All the various enterprises, agriculture, shops, industries, hotels, entertainment, etc., generate their own incomes. They each give a tenth of their total incomes to the central bank which is also managed by a committee of co-owners, and they share the rest equally among their members. If this arrangement causes headaches to any particular enterprise, it is an option to give a smaller contribution, or none at all. Even to say this is misleading, however, because there's no form of compulsion or mandatory requirement. If an enterprise is still in difficulty, which, again, is only a theoretical situation, it can get financial relief from the central bank; not as a loan, but as a grant.

Apart from being there as a safeguard against any financial problems in the different enterprises in the state, the central bank deals with arrangements about foreign currencies. It may also help, if the need arises, where public services, such as transport or health, are concerned. In addition, it has a special fund set aside to help any individuals who for some reason may not be able to work, or whose circumstances place financial burdens on them; all that they have to do is ask for whatever income they feel they need and that will be made available to them. (That's what your governments do to you through imposed systems of taxation; the utopians have neatly given power back to the people.) Should there be any difficulty about the fund not being adequate at any time to meet the requests for help, all the bank need do is ask for public subscriptions, which would be readily forthcoming. It may seem strange that people are automatically given what they feel they need, but there would never be any question of utopians asking for more or less than that.

X

In the modern world, and, of course, particularly in cities, the provision and regulation of transport are perennial problems. How do the utopians solve those problems without imposing any regulations?

Their solution is basically very simple. The fact that there are no centralized establishments, for example, governments (apart from the central bank), is a help towards having a fairly even spread of population throughout the state; nevertheless, there's still quite a heavy concentration of people in the cities. People don't bring their cars into the cities at all. This has happened entirely of their own volition. Some people take their cars, occasionally, to the outskirts of the cities to within walking distance of where they want to go. Different groups and/or individuals operate buses and coaches and taxicabs (again on a shared ownership basis, where applicable) and, because there is such free movement within the cities, there are no traffic jams. Travel is a speedy and pleasant experience. Small flying machines somewhat, on the style of helicopters, but more advanced in design, are popular, and becoming more so. Some utopians are concentrating on developing more sophisticated technological methods of flying so that the vast open air space can be utilized more efficiently for the benefit of the people (and without encroaching too much on birds' territory!).

There are also, of course, airplanes and trains managed on the usual basis. There's no competition between the different groupings since nobody is obsessed with making money and nobody is short of money; the primary motivation is to provide efficient service and to do so cheerfully.

There are some small hospitals, but because the people are living their lives in such relaxed and harmonious ways, they are generally in good health. Many of them like to meditate regularly by themselves or in groups. They are most attentive to preserving the serenity of their inner being, and that's reflected in their outer expression. Their countenances are open and friendly, and their smiles light up their eyes. Their doctors and nurses have studied and developed what are known as alternative or complementary healing techniques as well as what might be called orthodox medicine. Their services, both as teachers and as healers, are increasingly in demand in other countries, so that they are often absent from home for long periods. That's their own choice, of course.

Since there's no longer any formal government, how is utopia represented in relation to other countries, for example, embassies, visits by heads of state? Once again, through a committee system.

Because the utopians don't have rulers, there's nobody in a position, or charged with responsibility, to decide who will perform what function or, indeed, whether there's a function to be performed at all. People naturally gravitate towards their areas of interest and take whatever initiatives, and make whatever responses, they think are needed. Everything is done, every position is filled, by agreement. Understandably, this may seem like a haphazard and impractical way of ordering affairs of state. But isn't it essentially what democracy means? In any case, the utopians had already designed in spirit, before they came into Earth, the broad outline of what their roles were going to be in this new exploration in consciousness. Colleagues in spirit, who are not incarnating, are guiding them so that the density of the Earth vibration will not cloud their insight and interfere with their overall purpose.

I think I have said enough about the arrangements by which the state is managed for you to get the general picture.

XI

The utopians do not, in practice, have formal religious belief systems, although, of course, as is the case in spirit, there is complete freedom of religious expression. They accept their own divinity in their humanness and they are at one with God in them. To them God is not an external force to be worshipped but, rather, the center of their own being continually expressed both in themselves and in everybody and everything around them. They have come to unite, not to divide, and to help people to find that pot of gold at the end of the rainbow for which they are endlessly searching and which, of course, is reunion with God in them.

There are church buildings in utopia which people use for group discussions, adventures in spirit, meditations, talks, etc., as well as religious ceremonies, if desired. Some people like to savor the atmosphere and the peace of empty churches.

The utopians are fun-loving people. They love music, singing, dancing, parties, etc., according to their individual tastes. They have theaters, concert halls, cinemas, dance halls, sporting arenas, etc., which cater to varying interests (highbrow to lowbrow). Some of them enjoy alcohol, and occasionally overindulge, with predictable effects. They don't use drugs, other than for medicinal purposes.

Utopians are not sexually promiscuous since to them sexuality is linked to creative expression and intimacy. They enjoy their sexuality and they express it in all their activities. Because their work is satisfying, enjoyable, and fulfilling, no part of their creativity is suppressed.

There is no formal institution of marriage in utopia, in keeping with their ways of having no formalities of any kind; and, of course, they are manifesting on Earth as in spirit. Before they were born into physical bodies they made arrangements with their soul mates that they would meet and share sexual intimacy within the material sphere. They created family situations. They have their own houses or apartments, their own private worlds to the extent that they wish. Some of them have children (who will usually have come from the second rather than the fourth stage but are ready to move beyond the second stage).

You will probably have noticed that in the evolution of the twentieth century, sexual expression moved through phases of prudishness to what was known as free love, which was facilitated by the development of contraception. Sex qua sex became an end in itself. As the end of the century approached, however, it became more and more evident that many people wanted more than merely mechanical or physical sexual release. They were looking for an intimacy of communication as an integral ingredient in sexual intercourse. Women, for whom the century brought more freedom in the acknowledgment of their sexuality, have been at the forefront of the acceleration in the movement of consciousness; and, in the process, many of them found gaps opening up between themselves and their partners, if married or in like relationships; or between themselves, if they are heterosexual, and men generally, because men on the whole tended to be slower to move beyond purely rational or conditioned perspectives. So, as the twentieth century drew to a close, the search for intimacy became more pronounced, and the need for a new language or different communication in sexuality grew deeper.

In the utopia of 2030 the people are used to sexual intimacy. They enjoy sexual union uninhibitedly. They have no special interest in techniques, other than whatever is mutually pleasing. Their bodies are never occasions of shame to them. As I have already said, they are not sexually promiscuous, not due to any conditioned morality but because they don't believe that sexual intimacy can be achieved in that way.

They welcome children because they like them and also because it's an important part of their purpose that they are vehicles for souls to experience or re-experience physical life as a means of growing in consciousness. Before coming to Earth they made arrangements with the souls who will be born to them as children (and their guides), and these arrangements determine the number of children born to each couple. Some made no arrangements about having children, and some chose to have sexual intimacy with partners of their own gender. You understand that they see sexual expression as a means of helping intimacy of communication rather than in any mold of morality.

They make no moral judgments about contraception or abortion. They know that if they have made arrangements with souls to be born to them as children, those souls will be sure to come to them at the appropriate times; they trust that they will respond to the signals.

Children are much loved and are usually reared by their parents in their own homes. They are not given any specific religious training but they are imbued with the deep spirituality of their parents and teachers. They are aware of, and consciously communicate with, their guides/guardian angels, and they are also, at an early stage in their lives, helped by their parents to be aware of feelings of connectedness or unity with God in them.

Education is geared very much to individual preferences. Arrangements are made for children to be brought together on a coeducational basis, where they are taught by those who have chosen to do that work. There are no set methods of teaching, no competitive examinations; from an early age children are given opportunities to find and develop their own unique talents.

There's no peer group pressure nor is there any bar to possibilities for higher or expanded education. There are no requirements for formal qualifications, such as certificates, or diplomas, or degrees. The people are highly proficient and knowledgeable within their chosen fields, which include all known forms of human expression, as well as some pioneering ones. Learning is a constantly joyful experience. Career guidance presents no difficulties because creativity is never suppressed and there are always either existing openings for employment in a person's selected field, or he can easily create one. He will be both encouraged and helped to do so.

The utopian system, or no system, of education has become the envy of many observers, and the practice has grown of sending children and young adults from other countries to be trained by the utopian teachers. This is a development which is greatly welcomed in utopia and which is, of course, very much in line with the purpose of its existence. In due course the foreign students will, if they wish to do so, introduce aspects of the utopian ways into their own systems.

XII

Utopia has no army, no navy, no courts, no prisons, no police force. So is it open-house for invaders or robbers or lawlessness of whatever form? In your physical world, as it exists at present, there's a huge emphasis on security in all aspects of life, including personal safety, private property, and national boundaries. In spirit there's obviously no need for any of that. So the issue of security presents a forceful challenge to adventuring souls who wish to merge, to an advanced extent, the physical and spirit worlds.

In utopia itself, because of the people's level of awareness, there's no need for any security system since there is total respect for each person's being. Nobody would even think of imposing on another, or encroaching on another person's space, or taking what belongs to somebody else. But what's to stop another country invading utopia, or people from other places coming to rob and plunder, since there would be no physical preventative measures, apparently?

You may remember that I talked about how guides can keep your aura clear if you ask them to do so. I went on to explain that the way in which they do that is rather like an electric fence being placed around your aura so that any "invader" would experience something of a shock in trying to get through. The auras of the utopians are all protected in that way and the concentrated power of their positivity embraces the whole country. Any invaders with negative intentions would find themselves up against an intangible force which would be all the more effective because of not being visible nor, perhaps, understandable or explainable within the rationale of human conditioning. Yet it is true that utopia experiences no invasions of any kind, either private or national, nor does it anticipate any.

Here it is, I think, relevant to observe how what happens internally reflects itself externally. A person who lacks self-acceptance, which, in the final analysis, is due to separation from God, finds it necessary to try to create inner security by presenting a defensive mask to the world. The emphasis on external security systems is a projection of people's inner being.

XIII

Some people from other countries wish to go to live in utopia. Usually, they are people who are in tune in themselves with the utopian way and fit easily into the new lifestyle. There are no difficulties of overcrowding or overpopulation.

The communications media—newspapers, television, radio—play important roles in utopia. They are free to print or broadcast anything they like since there are no controls. That's also true, of course, where publications of any kind are concerned, such as, books, magazines, videos, tapes. They place great emphasis on expressing their creativity in whatever form it comes and they are usually very willing to share the fruits of that creativity with others. They don't go in for pornography in their literature or visual presentations, not from a moralistic standpoint but because they don't enjoy it. They don't isolate themselves from the rest of the world in any way, and, generally, they keep themselves well informed through the media about what's happening worldwide. People who are interested in communications have extensive scope for expressing themselves; anybody who wants to is free to publish his own newspaper, magazine, etc., or to set up his own television or radio station. In practice, all of these ventures are undertaken by cooperative effort with co-ownership.

Utopia inherited telephone and postal systems from the previous administrations. In line with what happens generally in the new state, routine operations are largely automated and the systems as a whole are overseen by committees who manage and co-own them. The users pay annual rental charges for both services; the modest rates are determined by the committees, and there are no charges for telephone calls or postage stamps or any of the telecommunications or postal services provided. The post offices which were already in place have continued to be used for the reception and distribution of mail, and also as collection points for any money which people receive from the central bank. Each post office makes its own arrangements with the bank.

XIV

All administrative procedures in utopia are simple, with no "red tape" and no form-filling. There is real democracy because the people cooperate with each other in a spirit of total harmony and nobody is seeking to control anybody else, or to be protected from anybody else. The people are secure in themselves individually, and that inner feeling spreads outwards and creates the environment in which they live.

Because all governmental and other institutional arrangements no longer exist, many people whose energies would formerly have been occupied in such employments as the civil service, courts, police, prisons, banks, insurance offices, were set free to express their creativity in ways which would reflect more truly their own personalities and styles. There are no "square pegs in round holes" in utopia. The state is not burdened with heavy administrative costs, which releases money for more creative purposes.

XV

Perhaps the thought enters your head that the picture I have been painting of a country which is all serenity and harmony and simplicity is one of unrelieved dullness? Where's the "buzz" that can be got from conflict, argumentation, juicy bits of gossip?

Those questions are, of course, as relevant to life in spirit as they are to life in our Earthly utopia. The fact is, that as souls regain their lost awareness their inner harmony increases. I think it's fair to say that people generally don't like to live in states of conflict. Usually, great stress is involved for people who are forced for one reason or another to live in discordant atmospheres. People who enjoy looking at films showing battles or wars don't want to be participants in such martial escapades. Equally, people who flock to see a play featuring dramatic conflicts in personal relationships don't want to have similar conflicts in their own lives. Or, people who avidly read thrillers which involve murders, or victimizations of different kinds, can become totally absorbed in the stories because they know that they don't have to relate to them in real life. Or, people can savor the cut and thrust of courtroom exchanges, although they would themselves shrink from such experiences in their own lives.

What happens as awareness increases is that people, if they wish, can enjoy conflict without having to experience it, for example, in movies, plays, books, sports. They can have the fun of participation without its pain. They can also participate, for example, in sports as much as they like, in the consciousness that they're playing games. They don't become namby pambies, they glow more in their being, they express themselves more openly and more vividly. They don't automatically agree with each other for the sake of agreement or compromise; they may, indeed, hold totally differing points of view on certain issues and strongly voice their opinions but without resentment, or defensiveness, or dogmatism, or seeking to impose their ideas in any way. In other words, what I'm trying to say is that they enjoy themselves thoroughly.

XVI

The question on which this chapter is based was, "What is life going to be like on planet Earth in the future?" I have attempted to answer the question by using an illustration of a new country which could serve as a model for the planet as a whole in a gradually evolving process. I have given you an outline with some, but not too much, detail.

Since it is true that we are all spirit beings, some of us temporarily in physical bodies and some of us not confined in that way, it is fitting, I think, that we should seek to understand each other better. So I have endeavored to bridge the gap between our worlds by making the world of spirit more real for you and easier to imagine. It is difficult to convey by description, which necessarily defines, the joy of life in spirit, particularly at the fourth stage and beyond. I hope we have succeeded, to some extent at least.

Is utopia a possibility, not just for a small section, but for all of the planet? Yes. It will obviously take a long time in your terms, and it will inevitably happen gradually. I have no doubt that it will happen. Then planet Earth will have fulfilled its purpose as a vehicle for regaining lost awareness and will truly be a divine playground.

This session on Utopia is an attempt to create a deeper understanding of life and all its potential, as well as to eliminate at least some of the controlling influences that have strangled so much of the adventuresome, exploratory spirit which is present, but too often suppressed, in all people.

I know that many people (particularly those who won't at present be interested in reading this book) would immediately dismiss the utopian way of life that I have described as totally unrealistic. Yet, already, millions of people throughout the world are moving in that direction, feeling that they have to get away from existing controlling systems, or to live with them without fulfillment. I'm not seeking to present you with a pipe dream. It is all eminently practical, with people's energies being used freely and constructively rather than defensively and often destructively.

I described a utopia in terms of a small country of about four million people. You wonder how the blueprint could work in the United States and even, for example, in such a huge city as New York. Is it conceivable that the enormous range of essential services could be organized without extensive hierarchical structures to administer them?

From a purely material standpoint the scale of what has been achieved in the United States in such a relatively short period of time is awe-inspiring; it illustrates clearly the creative potential in people when they have the scope to express it.

If I may use an illustration which may initially seem inappropriate but yet is very relevant, I ask you to imagine the magnitude of America, its towering skyscrapers, its seemingly never-ending motorways, its sheer breathtaking magnificence, and add in all the other continents which complete planet Earth, with all their diversities and complexities and immensities; and, also, take into account all the other planets, of which you know relatively little, other than that they're quite large. You still would not have an impression, even to the extent of the tiniest fraction, of the capacity of one soul, not to mention the infinity of God. All the same, you have a strong indication of what souls can do when they are united in a common purpose. Any community, any country, any continent, no matter how large, is a collection of individual souls. As they cooperate in expansion of consciousness, anything is possible. Human beings have shown in many ways, often regrettably destructive ones, what they can achieve. As they grow in increasing awareness of their divinity, there are no limits to what is achievable even within the human state.

Part V

Adventure in Spirit

Through the ages people have sought ways and means of transcending the limitations of the physical world. For example, some have concentrated their inventiveness in technological directions with remarkable results; others have developed their physical skills through, for instance, sporting achievement; still others have managed the seemingly extraordinary feat of appearing to be in two places at the same time (bilocation).

In your physical manifestation it's very difficult for you to accept or, indeed, understand that instant creation is a fact of life. In spirit terms there's no problem with that idea, at least as soon as a soul becomes accustomed to being "dead," because it's immediately obvious; as I have explained earlier, if a soul thinks of, or imagines, something, it manifests instantaneously (like rubbing a magic lantern). On the other hand, if you in your human state think of something, you usually have no immediate physical evidence of what's created by your thought. Yet creation follows from your thoughts in your human form as surely as it will when you leave the physical state.

What I propose to do in this session is to take you, with your agreement, while you are fully conscious and grounded, on an adventure which is designed to help you transcend the limitations of your present physical dimension and sample how the world of spirit works. You will not be going into trance or an out-of-body state; at all times you will be in full control and free to continue or discontinue the adventure as you wish.

Please bear in mind that in spirit you are beyond the boundaries of time and space, that there is no confinement and that anything is possible. All that's needed is that you're willing to participate in our adventure and to allow it to happen in whatever way it will. You don't have to worry about whether you have a hang-up about visualizations, or whether you're inclined to fall asleep when you try anything like this; just take it as it comes and I promise you that it will work for you at some level.

As always, in order to be more truly yourself, the more relaxed you are the better. The biggest barriers to relaxation are, invariably, thoughts, whether focused on a particular problem or situation or just chasing each other at random. It doesn't matter what form of relaxation you use as long as it suits you and it works. My suggestion, which you may find helpful, would be to sit comfortably, close your eyes, and breathe deeply in and out for a few minutes; don't fight or resist whatever thoughts come into your head (resistance always reinforces) and you'll find that they'll fade away, leaving you in a state of peaceful being.

Since what I am conveying to you needs to be embodied in words, and since you can't read with your eyes closed, in order to participate in the trip you'll need to prerecord what follows or to arrange to have somebody read it for you.

You have been notified that you have been given a gift of a trip to a location which is being kept secret from you, that all arrangements have been made to have your family, work, etc., looked after while you're away, that you have no need to worry about details of currency, clothes, travel, or accommodation.

Everything is organized so that you haven't a care in the world; all you need to do is to be ready to go at a particular time.

You are willing to accept the gift, and at the appointed time you see a magnificent looking limousine stopping outside your home. A man emerges from the car and comes to your front door. When you open the door he informs you that his name is Luke and that he has come to take you on the preliminary part of your adventure. He holds one of the rear doors of the car open for you and you recline into the plush seat. Luke starts the car and it glides smoothly along the road.

In front of you is a cabinet with a variety of drinks and some glasses. A card located prominently on the cabinet reads, "Please Help Yourself." You decide that you may as well sample what's offered and you do. You notice there's a television set in the cabinet and you switch it on if you feel inclined to do so. Luke thoughtfully leaves you to your own devices without interruption.

Time passes unobtrusively and comfortably. You have made up your mind not to wonder about where you're going, but just to enjoy the experience moment by moment. You are completely relaxed. Maybe you even let yourself savor the theatricality of waving royally to imaginary masses of cheering people as you elegantly pass by.

Hardly any time at all seems to have elapsed when you find that you have arrived at an airport runway. Luke stops the car, gets out and opens one of the rear doors, indicating to you that you're going to be traveling on the airplane sitting on the runway near the car.

A smiling young woman greets you and introduces herself as Angela. There's a red carpet leading from the plane to the door of the car. You are hesitant to believe that it was laid out specially for you, but yet that seems to be the case.

Ushered by Angela, you walk along the carpet and up into the plane. You see that there's no other passenger but yourself. The only crew members on the plane seem to be Angela and the captain, who introduces himself as Michael, welcomes you on board, and wishes you a pleasant trip. Angela informs you that you are, in fact, the only passenger so that you're free to choose whichever seat you prefer.

You are somewhat flabbergasted to learn that the whole plane is for you only and fleetingly you wonder has there been some mistake, that maybe all the special treatment is intended for some very important public person. As if she's reading your mind, Angela reassures you that there's no mistake; that, yes, the special treatment is for a very important person, and that you are that person. You joyfully experiment with the seats until you find what you like best.

Angela brings you a menu and asks you to choose what you'd like to eat, and she also offers you your choice of drinks. There's a luxury of choice from your favorite food and drinks. You make your selections and sit back, wallowing in the enjoyment of what's happening to you.

Easily and smoothly the plane takes off and you rejoice in the feeling of being airborne. Quickly the ground underneath recedes and all below looks smaller and smaller. Soon you're above the white cushion of clouds feeling that you're in a magical cocoon of blissful serenity.

Angela brings you a meal such as would make even the most fastidious gourmet's mouth water; a veritable feast designed to suit your palate. In the unaccustomed feeling of having no pressures of time you experience the meal and, then, replete and relaxed, you allow yourself to enjoy the freedom from day-to-day responsibilities and duties.

After some time, Angela comes to you and tells you that you're about to embark on another phase of your journey. You notice that the plane is coming to a stop, but it's not like the usual way of touching down on a runway; there's no sensation of descending or of contact with the ground.

Angela takes your hand and assures you that there's nothing to fear as she leads you towards the exit.

You step out onto what seems to be a ladder, but again you have no sensation of physical contact. As you reach the foot of the ladder you are surprised to find that you're apparently walking on solid ground but yet seemingly gliding over it.

Reassuringly, Angela stays with you and appears to be completely familiar with the conditions which you are now experiencing. For you, too, there's a familiarity about everything, but yet you feel different. You're not confined in your movements, there's a lightness about you; it's as if you're flying rather than walking, and you have a panoramic view of everything. It's all very beautiful and peaceful.

You ask Angela where are you. She smiles and answers enigmatically that you're not anywhere but that you're at home. You realize that that's all the information you're going to get from her, for the present at any rate, and you allow yourself to continue to be guided by her.

You have arrived at the entrance to a magnificent looking building. Angela leads you through a long hallway. As you go through the hallway you meet people, all of whom greet you familiarly. You notice that nobody seems to have to open doors, they all glide through them. You wonder idly why do they bother with doors at all; probably for appearance's sake, you think.

Soon the same thing happens to you and Angela; you reach a door and you both glide through it. You're in what seems like a vast library. Angela guides you to a particular section of the room and indicates to you to sit in an armchair. She makes a gesture and suddenly you're looking at a movie. The opening credits show you as the star, the producer and the director. As the movie unfolds you see yourself in different roles but you have no doubt that it's you in varying manifestations.

You stay with the movie, allowing it to unfold, knowing that there's no hurry. You may wish to "freeze" some parts of it to give yourself time to absorb a particular scene or scenes.

As the movie draws to a close you see yourself as you now are, and what you set out to accomplish in your life.

When you're ready, the picture fades and Angela takes your hand and leads you from the room.

As you're wondering, what next? Angela guides you through another door into a room which is occupied by three radiant looking beings. They smile at you and one of them invites you to sit with them, addressing you by name and saying "welcome back" to you. That doesn't sound odd to you as you feel at home in the room and in their company. Angela, of course, is also sitting with you.

It doesn't seem necessary to use language. It's as if you know automatically what you're communicating to each other. You sense immediately that they are happy to discuss with you the movie you have just seen. If you wish, ask for an evaluation of your progress to date.

If you have any special concerns about yourself and/or others, or if you have unfulfilled dreams, or if you just want to have a general chat about spiritual or material matters, this is a good opportunity for you to look for guidance.

When you feel that you've had enough discussion, you all sit silently in loving harmony savoring the unity and the joy of being.

After what may be a little while, or a long while, you gather from Angela that she will take you on the next part of your trip if you are ready to move. You realize that it's open to you to come and go as you wish. As you take your leave of them you understand from the other three occupants of the room that you will be in constant contact with each other according as you desire it.

Now Angela takes you through a long corridor into another room. She suggests to you that you lie on a bed in the center of the room. As you do, the bed molds itself into your shape and is wonderfully comfortable. You find the atmosphere in the room totally relaxing, with muted color combinations and soft background music.

You are suddenly aware that there are four angelic beings around you, one at your feet, one at your head, and one on each side of you. You understand from them that they are there to give you healing, if you so wish. You gladly accept.

Immediately you begin to feel a flow of energy through all parts of your body from the top of your head down to your toes.

As you radiate in the glow of the healing, impressions of the movie which you saw earlier may pass before you. In any case, whether they do or not, the healing which you are now receiving is ranging over your whole evolution since you separated yourself from your full awareness of yourself and of your place in God. You feel all the burdens, the suffering, the guilt, the weariness, the isolation, the sorrow of humanity lifted from you. You feel your love flowing from you towards yourself, towards all those you hold dear to you, and towards all souls; and you forgive yourself for all that followed from your act of separation from your own divinity. All the doubts fade away, there are no more questions to be asked, there's just the ineffable joy of being.

You feel a tap on your shoulder and you see Angela standing, smiling, beside you. You're no longer aware of the angelic beings. You send thoughts of profound gratitude to them and you rise and go with Angela.

Once again you pass through corridors, smilingly saluting those whom you meet.

You leave the building and soon you find yourself back at the entrance to the plane. Michael welcomes you aboard again, and, without delay, you're settled into your seat and the plane is smoothly on its way. You are still savoring all that you have experienced on your trip when the plane touches down. This time you can feel the contact with the ground and you know you're back on Earth.

You thank Angela and Michael, and both of them hug you lovingly as you realize that Luke is waiting for you beside the plane with the same limousine. You sit in the back seat and wave goodbye to Angela and Michael as the car moves easily away.

The homeward bound journey is more internalized and reflective than the outward one. Soon you're safely back at your front door. You thank Luke and you enter your home basking in the glow of your experience and realizing that the gift which you received is intended as a continuing one which is open to you to repeat whenever you wish to do so.

Part VI
Dialogue with Shebaka

Paddy: If it's okay with you I'd like to do some random exploration with you as well as to bring up questions that often seem to bother people.

Shebaka: Fine.

Paddy: One of the most common questions goes something like this: How can you say that there's no evil when there are so many examples all through the history of the planet, as we know it, of atrocities committed by some people against others? How can the perpetrators of such atrocities be regarded as divine, part of God? Is that tantamount to saying that God is evil as well as good?

Shebaka: Those questions, as you know, have figured prominently in our communications, but since they keep coming up it's well to look at them again. In my explanations I described the states of being as awareness and different degrees of non-awareness. In ultimate awareness souls are expressing their divinity fully. Until they reach that state they continue to cloak their divinity in expressions of non-awareness.

It's difficult for people not to take up positions in the immediacy of whatever presents itself to them. Of course I can't deny the awfulness of some of the things that people have done, and do, to each other as adults and to children and animals. When these actions are considered in isolation they can only be regarded as evil and the perpetrators similarly so.

But in spiritual terms nothing can be viewed in an isolationist context.

It's always easier to explain something by using a hypothetical example.

From an early age Philip got involved in criminal activities, such as mugging, robbery. As he grew into adulthood he had increasingly less compunction about injuring, sometimes severely, helpless people. It didn't bother him that from time to time he was apprehended and sentenced to terms of imprisonment. On release he resumed his criminal career with renewed vigor and cruelty, showing no vestige of compassion for any of his victims, whatever their circumstances.

However, in midlife, Philip was involved in a serious accident which left him completely immobilized for several months. Initially he was hospitalized and later he was taken care of by family members from whom he had earlier separated himself. During his convalescence a transformation took place in him. The kindness shown to him, by people for whom the question "what's in it for me?" had obviously no meaning, slowly began to make an impression on him. Feelings which he had hitherto suppressed started to surface in him. Suddenly people had individual identities rather than being regarded as potential victims. It nonplused him that it didn't seem to matter to the people around him that he had a reputation as a dangerous criminal. They treated him no differently from anybody else and even, unbelievably, with affection, although all that was hard for him to accept initially.

The outcome was that Philip decided to train as a physical therapist and has gone on to do wonderful healing work with people. He has become as dedicated in his new life as he had previously been in his old one.

Let's look at this case study in a twofold way.

If we take Philip himself first, I think it's easy to accept that he's not an evil man even though many people would have categorized him as such on the evidence of his criminal activities. In familiar human terminology it might be said that the capacity for evil in him was transformed into the capacity for good.

That still leaves us with his earlier actions which injuriously affected the lives of many people. How can they be regarded as other than evil? On one level, which is the immediate human one, they can't. But in spiritual terms there's always a broader perspective. I can't consider any question or any case without taking into account the continuity of soul, which means that whatever happens to any individual needs to be put into the context of that individual's journey as a soul. Put in that light it may well be that what would be regarded, in its immediacy, as evil would, in fact, be ultimately positive in its effects.

May I remind you that humanity is a temporary condition and that its purpose is to enable growth in awareness. At the risk of boring you I must repeat that all happenings are only important in the effects they create; and those effects can only be judged within the broad canvas of each individual's evolution.

It's important to mention, too, that some souls have chosen human manifestation in catalytic roles, and that's likely to be a continuing feature of human evolution as long as it's considered desirable. In that context the easier role is, you'll agree, that which is generally seen in a positive or often saintly light. But what of the soul who, in a human role, has elected to become the subject of public opprobrium for the purpose of acting as an agent of change in people's attitudes? There have been several such souls in human history who have been held up as symbols of infamy and evil but who, in the process, have influenced people towards looking into themselves and how they behave towards others. They are the unsung heroic beings. It's easy, for instance, to perform such a role in a play or a movie, where everybody knows that it's not "real life," but it's a different story when one doesn't have that cover.

A classic example is the role of Judas in the story of Jesus. Had it not been for the part played by Judas, whose name subsequently became synonymous with betrayal, the story could not have been recorded as it was. Was Judas evil, do you think? Were his actions evil? I hope you see that when the perspective is broadened there are no facile judgments or categorizations.

In Philip's case the transformation took place within his present lifetime. It's a fact that in many cases no such transformation has yet taken place, even after many physical lives; but it will, because each soul's divine nature cannot be suppressed indefinitely.

In an earlier session I used an analogy of the soul as an electric light bulb which, though switched on, is buried in earth and doesn't show any light. When the earth is removed from it the bulb shows all its light. It's the same bulb all the time. That's the process of evolution in a nutshell. The light is the divinity which is always there even when it's hidden. What you call evil is the earth of unawareness which ultimately falls away and the divine reality is then revealed in all its glory. The love that God is never rejects or abandons or separates itself from any soul; the soul itself is responsible for its separation.

Paddy: It seems that there's still a big gap in perceptiveness between our worlds. Is it possible to be more specific as to how the gap can be narrowed?

Shebaka: That very perceptiveness does not allow me to be more specific than I am. The human being is always looking for chapter and verse, for the maps that will pinpoint his direction for him in fine detail. That's not the way of spirit. In our sessions I attempted to paint a broad picture of life in spirit in the hope that that will help those who will have access to our books or who already have such access to integrate more fully their divinity with their humanness. Thus, as that integration happens, the gap will be closed.

Paddy: What, in your view, is the biggest single challenge facing humanity at present?

Shebaka: Facetiously, I might say not to ask questions like that! Seriously, I'd like to put the question another way: what's the biggest single challenge facing each human being at present? My answer is to attain freedom from all negative karmic effects through union with (God) the Father. Humanity as a global concept takes its significance from the individuals who comprise it. As each individual finds inner completeness and peace, the problems of humanity will be proportionately diminished. No revolution, no organization, no religion, no system, will provide adequate solutions, as should be obvious at this stage of evolution. Global or generic answers could only be effective if people were to be standardized, like robots. That's why utopia will have no prescribed formulas.

Paddy: That's why too, partly at least I think, you don't favor gurus?

Shebaka: It depends on what's meant by gurus. While it's true that each soul ultimately has to find or rediscover its own truth, the help that's available through the interlinking of consciousness in all souls is a hugely significant factor in growth of awareness. Because souls are at different levels of awareness those at lower levels have much to gain from interaction with those at higher levels.

Difficulties have arisen in the human evolution when some people have set themselves up, or have been set up, as the custodians of absolute truth and have dogmatically declared that the way to salvation is only possible through faithful adherence to that "truth." Sadly, such absolutism has attracted millions of devotees throughout human history, and has led to all sorts of fanatical excesses. Any belief or practice which inhibits people's free will, or seeks to impose itself on them or control them through confining them within behavioral prescriptions, is spiritually damaging.

But, of course, there are teachers and pupils and there will continue to be a need for teachers for as long as the need for the human condition exists. I have stressed the all-important role of education, in a vastly more extended and individually oriented format than it exists at present, in solving the problems of the world. The role of the teacher or guru is ideally that of a facilitator who provides a platform through which pupils will find their individually unique ways and truths which may or may not be similar to those of the teacher.

So, to answer your question; if the word "guru" can be taken to mean an empowering teacher rather than somebody who seeks to attract devotees, I have no difficulty with it.

Paddy: Even when one accepts unreservedly how significant spiritually is non-interference with free will, it's still very difficult to see how that can be put into practice fully in the human state. We came up against this dilemma in discussing criminal activities and responses to them.

Shebaka: I understand. But there is free will or there isn't. Once you accept that each soul (whether in spirit or temporary human manifestation) has free will, it follows that any enforced restriction of that, whether by a system or by an individual, has damaging spiritual effects on both parties. If you start bringing in qualifying considerations, such as, "I agree with the notion of free will in principle, but in practice it has to be subordinated to the common good"; or, "Free will is a great thing but you have to draw the line somewhere"; or, "Nobody has the right to do wrong," you're now subject to the vagaries of changing perceptions of "common good" or "right" or "wrong" and to the potential for abuse inherent in those perceptions, such as those promulgated by self-proclaimed representatives of all "right thinking people"—whoever they may be!

Paddy: Recently I heard about a "Shabaka stone" in the British Museum, and subsequently I read that this stone relates to a King Shabaka who reigned in Egypt from 712 to 698 B.C., and who, having discovered that material on which the story of creation according to the god Ptah had been written had been partially destroyed by worms, arranged that the surviving part of it should be carved in stone in order to preserve it; hence the Shabaka stone. Was that you in one of your incarnations?

Shebaka: Yes, it was. I thought it important that the material, such as it was in its extant form, should be available for future generations. Let's hope that the record of our communications will prove to be more durable! Incidentally, isn't there a neat symbolic irony about some of the material having been eaten by worms?

I chose to use that name in our communications because it seemed to me to have an appropriateness in the context of what we are endeavoring to achieve. I didn't reveal the historical connection to you at the outset because it would have personalized (or humanized) me too much as far as you were concerned.

Paddy: I found it helpful initially that the name had no associations for me. I didn't attempt to put a shape on you or to identify you in terms of gender.

Since our communication has been a two-way process, which for its clarity and accuracy has been dependent on my use of words, I'd like to check with you again at this stage whether the books are a true record of all the material conveyed by you.

Shebaka: Words are a form of structure. Human affairs are ordered through structure. Communication in the human state relies to a large extent on the structure of language. It is extremely difficult to convey the notion of spirituality in terms of structure since it doesn't know structure. The challenge for us is to provide an understanding of spirituality in a way that will be humanly comprehensible. Insofar as words could do that, I'm happy that the books convey accurately the substance of my communications.

Paddy: I know that in some of our sessions you outlined in quite a lot of detail what life in spirit is like, and the reasons why it's not desirable that communication between the spirit and physical states should be generally evidentially obvious. In my own case I have, from time to time, pleaded for clearer indications that I was connecting with you rather than talking to myself. Because the material in the communications made so much sense to me, the need for more obvious proof of your existence diminished. And, as you said, even if I could get all sorts of physical proof, it wouldn't be of any use to anybody else insofar as acceptance of the material was concerned. So I settled on trust and I'm happy with that.

When I move off this "mortal coil" though, suppose I want to have a chat with you; how can that be arranged?

Shebaka: Exactly as it is now; just send a thought to me and, hey presto! Here I am or there I am, whatever you like.

Paddy: But how different will it be? For example, I'll be able to see you, won't I? What will you look like? And what will I look like?

Shebaka: Yes, you'll be able to see me.

When the human state was designed, the physical framework was based on how souls appear to each other in spirit. There are no deformities, of course; the deformities evolved in physical appearance for various reasons which we have already explored.

Souls may choose to manifest as male or female, whichever they wish. When souls progress beyond the third stage of evolutionary growth, gender distinction doesn't apply, but some souls like to regard themselves as female and others as male. It all makes for variety.

In whatever way a soul chooses to manifest, once it progresses beyond the third stage it will always be radiant and beautiful. And, there's no aging.

Paddy: Perhaps you would elaborate a little on that.

As I understand the reincarnational process, in physical lifetimes the choice of gender is governed or, at least, influenced by a soul's purpose in a particular lifetime. I gather from what you're saying that that process continues, although obviously in a different way, in the spirit state?

Shebaka: As you know, the physical state is intended as a platform for transformation, with the objective of balancing feelings and thoughts and allowing a soul's divinity to express itself; or, put another way, releasing all negative karmic effects. Because of the ways in which male and female roles evolved in the expression of free will, it usually transpired that the balance could potentially be more easily attained through diversification between the gender manifestations.

The situation is broadly the same at the second and third stages in spirit.

Once a soul moves into the fourth stage, and beyond that, the balance is already there so that then a soul's choice is usually based on whatever sort of continuing expression it would like to have.

I know that there are all sorts of tensions, as well as intimately loving bonds, between the sexes, and that marriage and similar types of relationship are often beset by intense conflicts; but again, all that is a consequence of how free will has been exercised in human evolution. Whatever the tensions, it's nice, isn't it, that there are the two sexes, even for those who have chosen to express themselves in intimate relationship with the same gender as themselves.

Paddy: It's probably a stupid question, but are you glad that you won't be experiencing the human state again?

Shebaka: At least you didn't ask me to agree that it's a stupid question. You wouldn't expect me to be judgmental!

Yes, I am glad. However, I want to add that the potential for happiness in the physical world is enormous and is realizable; not only that, but I'm certain that the planet is evolving towards its paradisal expression.

Paddy: Will it continue to exist, then, indefinitely?

Shebaka: Not as you know it. It will go through much transformation and will become what I have chosen to call utopia because of the meaning associated with that word. All that's a long way off, unfortunately, but the good news is that it's already set on its course.

Paddy: I want to bring up just one other matter with you having to do with the fact that in recent years, as part of the new wave of consciousness, established structures, particularly religious ones, have been breaking down, and for many people they are no longer the symbols of security they once were. In my experience many people are finding it difficult to manage without the "maps" that were previously available and acceptable to them, even in their paternalistic wrapping. I know that over and over again you have reminded us of the help that's available to us if we're prepared to receive it, as we struggle along our individual paths, but still there can be a somewhat overwhelming sense of isolation sometimes. Would you like to say anything more about all that?

Shebaka: I sympathize with people who are feeling temporarily marooned. There's security of a kind in being given a set of rules and promised that if you obey them you'll be rewarded with eternal happiness in a specific location, heaven. When the rules are removed and you're informed that there's no location, as such, what can you hold on to? Solidity has disappeared into formlessness.

The whole point is, of course, that letting go of all the peripheral frameworks brings one face to face with oneself. As it's a fact that you're unique, as each individual is, and that's something that's beyond question, you know that there's nobody in existence who is exactly the same as you, how can you fit into a common mold? Isn't it a fair assumption that no matter how much you might admire, or even envy, another or others you wouldn't want to be anybody else?

What more can I say to you now than I have already said? Please enjoy the wonder of being unique and yet always linked to the loving energy, God, that animates the whole universe. How could you ever be yourself if you had to live eternally within a prescribed set of rules? What could be more marvelous than that you have in store for you the freedom of the whole universe, with nobody to say to you that you shouldn't be this or you shouldn't do that; that however you are and in whatever way you want to express yourself is entirely a matter for yourself, and that you can share yourself and your joy in life with whomsoever you wish?

Maybe you're in an interim state which is, at times, somewhat confusing and things get on top of you sometimes. But don't forget that there's always somebody to hold your hand; not to walk for you, but to help you to walk. You're free to create your own map, and it will be a masterpiece, have no doubt of that. And it won't be like any map you've ever seen or known because it will have no boundaries and no fixed coordinating points. These comments apply to everybody. When I say "you" in this, the concluding statement, I mean it in a general way also.

In the physical sense you are conditioned to endings. For example, it's normal for you to talk of projects as being unfinished, whatever that might mean! I hope you will take it for granted that the continuity of our communication will not be broken. You may like to know that whenever you dip into either of the books, even if only for a few moments, you are connecting with me if you wish to do so. That doesn't mean that I'm seeking to intrude in any way on your relationship with your guides and/or your oversoul. We operate in harmony with each other, as I'm sure you'd expect.

Never before in the history of the planet have so many people's energies been focused on peace, with the infinite support of all of us in spirit who are similarly motivated. You have no idea of the power that's generated by the energy emanating from even one person; please don't undervalue how important your contribution is. It doesn't matter whether you are in a central position of obvious influence or in what may seem like an obscure backwater. When your starting point is finding peace within yourself and when you link with all the evolved loving energy of the universe, whether along the lines of my earlier suggestions or in whatever way feels best to you, the effect is astronomical. It's difficult for you to conceive of that because you have no obvious evidence to confirm it for you, so for the present I hope you'll be prepared to accept my assurance that it is so.

In the communications which form the substance of these books, I have endeavored to provide facts and concepts and suggestions with the object of giving you a greater understanding of the whole scheme of life, and ways of finding ever increasing fulfillment and happiness in your own expression.

I make no demands on your acceptance of the material; it would be highly presumptuous and interfering of me to do so. Above all, I hope that our journey together to this stage has been helpful for you in finding your way and your truth.

I appreciate very much your patience and your trust. It has been, is, I should say, a great joy and privilege for me to have the honor of being with you in such an intimate way. My love and best wishes are with you always.

Conclusion

To all those who read these books, and to all those who don't, I wish joy and happiness and a speedy return to full awareness.

Appendix

The Cathar Prophecy of 1244 A.D.: That the church of love would be proclaimed in 1986

It has no fabric, only understanding.

It has no membership save those who know they belong.

It has no rivals, because it is noncompetitive.

It has no ambition, because it seeks only to serve.

It knows no boundaries for nationalisms are unloving.

It is not of itself, because it seeks to enrich all groups and religions.

It acknowledges all great teachers of all the ages who have shown the truth of love.

Those who participate practice the truth of love in all their beings.

There is no walk of life or nationality that is a barrier.

Those who are, know.

It seeks not to teach, but to be, and, by being, enrich.

It recognizes that the way we are may be the way of those around us because we are that way.

It recognizes the whole planet as a being of which we are a part.

It recognizes that the time has come for the supreme transmutation, the ultimate alchemical act of conscious change of the ego into a voluntary return to the Whole.

It does not proclaim itself with a loud voice but in the subtle realms of loving.

It salutes all those in the past who have blazoned the path but have paid the price.

It admits no hierarchy or structure, for no one is greater than another.

Its members shall know each other by their deeds and being and by their eyes, and by no other outward sign save the fraternal embrace.

Each one will dedicate their life to the silent loving of their neighbor, the environment, and the planet, whilst carrying out their task, however exalted or humble.

It recognizes the supremacy of the great idea which may only be accomplished if the human race practices the supremacy of love.

It has no reward to offer either here or in the hereafter save that of the ineffable joy of being and loving.

Each shall seek to advance the cause of understanding, doing good by stealth, and teaching only by example.

They shall heal their neighbor, their community and our planet.

They shall know no fear and feel no shame, and their witness shall prevail over all odds.

It has no secret, or arcanus, no initiation save that of true understanding of the power of love and that, if we want it to be so, the world will change, but only if we change ourselves first.

All those who belong, belong, they belong to the church of love.

About the Author:

Paddy McMahon was born in 1933 in County Clare in the west of Ireland, and has lived in Dublin since 1952. Employed in the Irish Civil Service from 1952 until 1988, he became aware that he and all people had spirit guides—guardian angels—and that we can communicate with them if we so choose. These communications, which began in 1978, have continued, and have inspired him to become increasingly involved in spiritual counseling and lecturing. Paddy's first communications from the highly-evolved spiritual being Shebaka began in 1981.

Hampton Roads Publishing Company

. . . for the evolving human spirit

Hampton Roads Publishing Company
publishes books on a variety of subjects,
including metaphysics, health, integrative medicine,
visionary fiction, and other related topics.

For a copy of our latest catalog, call toll-free
(800) 766-8009, or send your name and address to:

Hampton Roads Publishing Company, Inc.
1125 Stoney Ridge Road
Charlottesville, VA 22902

e-mail: hrpc@hrpub.com
Website: www.hrpub.com